FEED YOUR FAMILY RIGHT!

R E D U C E D ~~LOW-FAT~~ ~~LOW-SALT~~ **C A L O R I E S**

HEALTHY CHICKEN

BARBARA CHERNETZ

In consultation with Lynne Hill, R.D.

A JOHN BOSWELL ASSOCIATES/
KING HILL PRODUCTIONS BOOK

A Fireside Book
Published by Simon & Schuster

New York London Toronto Sydney
Tokyo Singapore

ACKNOWLEDGMENTS

I would like to thank Anne Salisbury of R. C. Auletta & Co., Perdue Farms' public relations agency in New York and the National Broiler Council for their help and assistance with facts and figures.

I also want to thank my mom, a great cook, for her inspiration, support and encouragement, and the rest of my family and friends, who never tired of tasting chicken.

A John Boswell Associates/King Hill Productions Book

Fireside
Simon & Schuster Building
Rockefeller Center
1230 Avenue of the Americas
New York, NY 10020

FIRESIDE and colophon
are registered trademarks
of Simon & Schuster, Inc.

Design by Nan Jernigan/The Colman Press

Printed and bound in the United States of America
1 3 5 7 9 10 8 6 4 2

Library of Congress Cataloging-in-Publication Data

Chernetz, Barbara.
Healthy chicken/Barbara Chernetz.
    p.   cm.—(Feed your family right)
"A Fireside book."
"A John Boswell Associates/King Hill Productions book."
ISBN 0–671–72898–9: $9.95
1. Cookery (Chicken)   I. Title.   II. Series.
TX750.5.C45C44   1991
641.6'65—dc20   90–24205
                CIP

CONTENTS

INTRODUCTION

Is it any wonder that chicken has so rapidly become our most popular food? Not only is it inherently good for you, it is economical, versatile, cooks quickly and easily, adapts to every variety of preparation and is a perfect foil for an infinite number of flavors.

The single most important reason, however, for chicken's growing popularity is its nutritional value. A 3½-ounce portion of skinless white meat chicken contains only 150 calories, about 30 percent less than beef and pork. Yet this same 3½-ounce portion contains 31 grams of protein, or about half the daily adult requirement, as well as being a source of Vitamin A, thiamin, riboflavin, niacin and hard-to-come by minerals, iron, zinc, phosphorus and calcium.

It's important to remember, though, that how chicken is prepared, what parts are used and which ingredients it is combined with can greatly affect its overall nutritional value. (A dark meat thigh with skin in a sauce with heavy cream more than counteracts chicken's natural benefits.) This book, therefore, maximizes the nutritional assets of chicken, and that is what sets it apart from other chicken cookbooks.

In most of the recipes, skinless, boneless chicken meat is called for. When it isn't (in Chapter 9 — Cornish Game Hens) simply remove the skin of the Cornish hens before eating to lower the calories and fat. When a recipe calls for cooked, shredded or diced chicken, it refers to skinless, boneless white meat. In most cases, 3 to 4 ounces of chicken are considered an appropriate serving portion.

When a vegetable oil is called for in the recipes, it's either a polyunsaturated one, such as canola or safflower oil, which tends to lower total serum cholesterol, or a monounsaturated one, such as olive oil, which has the added benefit of helping to reduce LDL, or "bad" cholesterol.

How you cook chicken is as important as the parts used and the sauces served with it. Low-fat cooking techniques, such as broiling, grilling, poaching, sautéing, stir-frying and microwaving, have been employed throughout the book.

What you cook chicken in is also crucial to maintaining its high nutritional profile. When cooking with very little fat, it's essential to invest in a good heavy nonstick skillet. Other cooking equipment good to have on hand is nonstick baking pans and saucepans.

I've also tried to elevate chicken's nutritional benefits by pairing it with other healthy ingredients such as grains, pasta, beans, sauces and relishes with little or no fat, and dressings that are based on nonfat yogurt and buttermilk, which are naturally low in fat.

Another special feature in this book is a chapter devoted just to kids. It's full of fun, simple recipes that kids of all ages will love to eat and you'll enjoy preparing, all guaranteed to become family favorites.

In addition, there are elegant appetizers, down-home hors d'oeuvres, splendid soups and sandwiches of an international variety, spectacular salads that go beyond the basic deli-style chicken salad, as well as favorite classics updated.

Look for tips throughout the book on the buying, handling, storing and cooking of chicken, as well as nutritional aspects.

This timely collection of healthy, innovative delicious chicken recipes fits in with today's life-style for the entire family and provides a cornerstone for good eating for the future.

Barbara Chernetz

NUTRITIONAL GUIDELINES

In recent years, many health organizations have made strong recommendations about the American diet. What seems to be common to all of them are the five following general principles of healthy eating for adults and older children.

▲ Achieve and maintain desirable body weight.
▲ Eat a nutritionally adequate diet consisting of a variety of foods.
▲ Reduce consumption of fat, especially saturated fats, and cholesterol.
▲ Increase consumption of complex carbohydrates and fiber.
▲ Reduce sodium intake.

Following are the specific nutritional guidelines that relate to these principles:

CALORIES—A measure of the energy available to the body from any food. The ideal daily caloric intake varies significantly depending upon age, sex, body type and activity level. It is the number of calories it takes to maintain your ideal weight. An average adult woman, for example, might need 1,500 calories a day to maintain her weight, while a large, active man might require 2,400 a day; someone trying to lose weight might have to restrict themselves to a mere 1,200 calories.

PROTEIN—Made of amino acids, the "building blocks" of the body, protein is essential to allow growth and repair of cells and to maintain optimum body functions. As important as it is, most Americans consume far more protein, and consequently more calories and often more cholesterol and saturated fats, than they need. Protein has 4 calories per gram, and it is recommended that only 15 to 20 percent of your daily calories come from protein.

TOTAL FATS—Fats provide the most concentrated source of calories at 9 calories per gram. Although the body needs a small amount of fat for energy and to help absorb oil-soluble vitamins, most of us eat far more fat than we need. Calories from all fats should be limited to no more than 30 percent of the calories ingested in a day. The following table relates fat intake to calories following this 30 percent guideline.

Daily Calories	Total Fat Maximum gm	Saturated Fat Maximum gm
2,400	80	26
2,000	66	22
1,800	60	20
1,500	50	16
1,200	40	13
1,000	33	11

(Recommendations are according to the American Dietetic Association, the American Heart Association and the National Cancer Institute.)

SATURATED FATS — Saturated fats are found in foods from animals, such as meat, poultry and eggs, in whole-milk dairy products and butter, and in palm oil, palm kernel oil and coconut oil, often used in processed foods. Product labeling can be misleading, because while a food might be touted as having no cholesterol, it may contain one of these saturated fats, which also tend to raise the blood cholesterol level. It is the total nutritional profile of a product or recipe that counts. Intake of saturated fats should be limited to no more than 10 percent of daily calories (see chart above).

CHOLESTEROL — Dietary cholesterol is found only in foods from animal sources. Our own bodies also manufacture cholesterol. There is strong medical evidence that reducing the intake of cholesterol and fats, especially saturated fats, helps to lower cholesterol levels in the blood. An average healthy adult should eat no more than 300 milligrams of cholesterol a day.

CARBOHYDRATES — These are the sugars and starches that provide our bodies with energy and dietary fiber. Simple sugars, which we get from foods like cookies, candies and sweeteners, are quickly digested and pass into the bloodstream, where they boost the blood sugar level, which then falls off rapidly. They offer little more than energy. Complex carbohydrates usually include starches, which may contain vitamins, minerals, fiber and some protein. They are broken down more gradually and assimilated slower, so that blood sugar levels remain more stable. We get complex carbohydrates from fruits, vegetables and grains, and most Americans need to add more of these to their diet. Carbohydrates contain 4 calories per gram, and it is recommended that they comprise 50 to 60 percent of our daily calories.

SODIUM — Sodium is found naturally in many foods; in balance with potassium, it helps regulate cell integrity and is linked to blood pressure. Excess sodium intake provides no known benefit and in some people may be linked to high blood pressure and cardiovascular disease. Consequently, the National Research Council of the National Academy of Sciences recommends that even healthy adults limit their sodium intake to a maximum of 2,400 milligrams a day, while the American Heart Association allows up to 3,000.

DIETARY FIBER — This is the structural part of plants also known as "roughage" or "bulk." There are two different kinds of fiber — soluble, which can be digested, and insoluble, which passes through the digestive system largely untouched. Fiber helps prevent constipation, aids in stabilizing blood sugar levels in diabetics, may prevent certain types of cancer and has been shown to help lower blood cholesterol levels when used in conjunction with a low-fat diet. Recommended levels of fiber are 20 to 35 grams per day.

As appealing as a healthy diet sounds and as simple as these prescribed guidelines appear at first glance, they are often confusing, because the percentages given are on a daily basis, which makes them difficult to utilize meal by meal, especially since actual recommended amounts vary dramatically depending on sex, age, weight and body type.

In general, the best way to eat a healthier diet is to change your eating habits to include more complex carbohydrates and less saturated fats and sodium. The following recipes, each with its own nutritional breakdown of calories, protein, total fat, saturated fat, cholesterol, carbohydrates and sodium, have been customized to assure healthy eating.

Many of the recipes are packed with vitamins and minerals, as well. Whenever a recipe contains over 20 percent of the U.S. Recommended Daily Allowance of a valuable vitamin or mineral, we've highlighted it on a bar graph below. Recipes that are not as high in these particular nutrients are also included because they contain a healthy balance of protein, fats and carbohydrates for the number of calories, and they are low in sodium and cholesterol.

The recipes in this book all come in at no more than 525 calories; all but a few are below 500. They allow a maximum of 800 milligrams of sodium and 125 milligrams of cholesterol; most contain much less. Except where otherwise noted, all calorie and other nutritional counts are per serving. Where an odd number of servings, such as 5, is listed, the recipe could serve a range, from 4 to 6. Nutritional counts have been rounded off to the nearest whole number.

—Lynne Hill, R.D.

BEST BEGINNINGS

Hors d'oeuvres are usually a prelude to whet the appetite for the main course that follows. But hors d'oeuvres can be more than snappy starters to a sit-down dinner. They can make substantial snacks, funky finger foods, perfect pass-arounds or elegant appetizers at a cocktail party.

Using different parts of the chicken, with all its different shapes and textures, produces an imaginative variety of appetizers.

The delicate phyllo puffs are small crisp bundles filled with a ground chicken and mushroom mixture in a light flaky pastry that uses vegetable cooking spray instead of melted butter to moisten the layers. At the other end of the spectrum are the down-home Buffalo chicken wings, sautéed, not fried, in very little oil and served with a blue cheese dressing, but this one has low-cal, low-fat buttermilk and yogurt as its base.

An inventive selection of sit-down/stand-up delectable hors d'oeuvres rounds out the chapter.

Sesame Chicken Nuggets with Peanut Dipping Sauce

4 SERVINGS

2 tablespoons smooth peanut butter
2 tablespoons reduced-sodium tamari or soy sauce
2 tablespoons rice wine vinegar or distilled white vinegar
½ teaspoon Asian sesame oil
½ teaspoon crushed hot pepper flakes
1 pound skinless, boneless chicken breasts, cut into 1½-inch pieces
2 tablespoons sesame seeds

1. In a small bowl, combine the peanut butter, tamari, vinegar, sesame oil and hot pepper flakes. Stir until blended. Set the peanut sauce aside.
2. Coat a large nonstick skillet with vegetable cooking spray and heat over medium heat. Add the chicken and cook, stirring frequently, until lightly browned outside and white throughout but still juicy, 4 to 6 minutes.
3. Toss with the sesame seeds to coat. Place a toothpick in each nugget and serve with the peanut sauce.

Calories: 212   Protein: 30 gm   Total Fat: 9 gm
Saturated Fat: 1 gm   Cholesterol: 66 mg   Carbohydrates: 3 gm
Sodium: 473 mg

A SUPER SOURCE OF:
Phosphorus ━━━━━━ 29%
Niacin ━━━━━━━━━━━━━━━ 72%

0%   U.S. Recommended Daily Allowance   100%

Buffalo Chicken Wings with Blue Cheese Dressing

Usually deep-fried and tossed in a melted butter hot sauce, this version of the classic wings is browned in a minimal amount of oil, which has been flavored with a hot red pepper sauce. 6 SERVINGS

¼ cup all-purpose flour
¼ teaspoon salt
¼ teaspoon freshly ground pepper
¼ teaspoon cayenne pepper
2 pounds chicken wingettes or wings, separated, wing tips discarded
2 teaspoons vegetable oil
1 tablespoon hot pepper sauce
4 celery ribs, halved lengthwise and cut into 3-inch pieces
Blue Cheese Dressing (recipe follows)

1. On a flat plate, combine the flour, salt, ground pepper and cayenne. Toss to blend. Dust the chicken wings with the seasoned flour to coat completely; shake off any excess.
2. In a large nonstick skillet, heat the oil and hot pepper sauce over medium-high heat. Add the wings and cook, stirring constantly, until browned all over and cooked through, 12 to 15 minutes. Serve with the celery pieces on the side and the blue cheese dressing for dipping.

Blue Cheese Dressing
MAKES ABOUT ¾ CUP

½ cup buttermilk
¼ cup nonfat plain yogurt
2 ounces blue cheese, crumbled
¼ teaspoon salt
¼ teaspoon freshly ground pepper

In a small bowl, combine all the ingredients. Stir until blended to a chunky consistency.

Calories: 250	Protein: 19 gm	Total Fat: 16 gm
Saturated Fat: 5 gm	Cholesterol: 56 mg	Carbohydrates: 7 mg
Sodium: 477 mg		

*B*randied Chicken Pâté

MAKES ABOUT 4 CUPS

1 eggplant (about 1¼ pounds)
1 tablespoon olive oil
½ cup chopped shallots
1 garlic clove, chopped
1 tablespoon all-purpose flour
1 pound ground chicken
2 teaspoons chopped fresh thyme or ½ teaspoon dried
1 teaspoon ground allspice
1 teaspoon salt
1 teaspoon freshly ground pepper
¼ cup no-salt chicken broth
3 tablespoons Cognac or brandy
1 teaspoon unflavored gelatin
Crackers or rounds of French bread, as accompaniment

1. Preheat the broiler. Pierce the eggplant once or twice and broil 4 inches from the heat, turning until charred all over, about 15 minutes. Let stand until cool enough to handle, then peel and reserve the eggplant.
2. Meanwhile, in a large nonstick skillet, heat the oil over medium heat. Add the shallots and garlic and cook, stirring, until softened, about 3 minutes. Stir in the flour and cook 1 to 2 minutes. Add the chicken and cook, breaking up any lumps with the back of a spoon, until no longer pink, about 5 minutes. Stir in the thyme, allspice, salt and pepper. Add the chicken broth and cook until the liquid is absorbed, about 5 minutes.
3. In a food processor, puree the eggplant and chicken mixture until smooth. Blend in the Cognac. Spoon into a 1-quart serving dish.
4. In a small bowl, sprinkle the gelatin over ¼ cup cold water. Let stand 2 to 3 minutes until softened. Place over simmering water and stir occasionally until dissolved. Pour the dissolved gelatin over the pâté and refrigerate until cold and set, several hours or overnight. Serve with crackers.

Calories: 18 per tablespoon	Protein: 1 gm	Total Fat: 1 gm
Saturated Fat: 0 gm	Cholesterol: 6 mg	Carbohydrates: 1 gm
Sodium: 41 mg		

Smoked Chicken Quesadillas with Red and Yellow Salsa

Leftover shredded cooked chicken can be substituted for the smoked chicken. MAKES 16 APPETIZERS

16 red and/or yellow cherry tomatoes, quartered and
  seeded
⅓ cup finely diced red and/or yellow bell pepper
¼ cup chopped scallions
1 tablespoon chopped fresh coriander or parsley
1 garlic clove, minced
1 small jalapeño pepper, seeded and minced
4 (7-inch) flour tortillas
4 ounces smoked chicken, cut into thin strips
2 ounces reduced-fat Monterey Jack cheese, grated

1. Preheat the oven to 350 degrees. In a small bowl, combine the tomatoes, bell pepper, scallions, coriander, garlic, jalapeño pepper and 1 tablespoon water. Stir the salsa to blend.
2. Place each tortilla on a sheet of foil. Sprinkle the chicken and cheese over the tortillas, dividing evenly. Fold each tortilla in half and press the edges together. Fold the foil over and seal the edges. Bake until the cheese is melted, about 5 minutes. Remove the tortillas from the foil and cut each into 4 wedges. Serve with the salsa.

Calories: 44 per quesadilla   Protein: 4 gm   Total Fat: 2 gm
Saturated Fat: 1 gm   Cholesterol: 9 mg   Carbohydrates: 4 gm
Sodium: 127 mg

*T*uscan Toasts with Smoked Chicken, Sundried Tomatoes and Fontina Cheese

MAKES 20 TOASTS

10 sun-dried tomato halves
1 loaf of Italian bread, cut into ½-inch slices
1 garlic clove, halved
1 tablespoon extra-virgin olive oil
2 ounces thinly sliced smoked chicken
4 ounces reduced-fat Fontina or mozzarella cheese, grated
  (about 1 cup)

1. Heat a small saucepan of water to boiling. Add the sun-dried tomatoes and cook until softened, about 2 minutes. Drain, then cut the tomatoes in half lengthwise.

2. Preheat the oven to 400 degrees. On a large baking sheet, toast the bread slices, turning once, until lightly browned, about 15 minutes. Remove from the oven; let cool slightly. Rub one side of each slice with the cut garlic. Brush with the olive oil.

3. Preheat the broiler. Layer the smoked chicken, sun-dried tomatoes and cheese on the toast slices. Broil 4 inches from the heat until the cheese is melted, 1 to 2 minutes. Serve hot.

Calories: 93 per toast	Protein: 4 gm	Total Fat: 2 gm
Saturated Fat: 1 gm	Cholesterol: 6 mg	Carbohydrates: 14 gm
Sodium: 188 mg		

*N*achos with Chicken and Cheese

Oven baking tortillas offers a low-fat, healthy alternative to the traditional method of frying them in lard or oil. MAKES 2½ DOZEN

5 (5½-inch) corn tortillas, cut into 6 wedges each
¾ teaspoon chili powder
1 teaspoon vegetable oil
⅓ cup chopped onion
1 garlic clove, minced
½ teaspoon ground cumin
½ pound ground chicken
½ cup mild enchilada sauce
15 thin slices pickled jalapeño pepper, halved
4 ounces reduced-fat Cheddar or Monterey Jack cheese, grated
⅔ cup nonfat plain yogurt

1. Preheat the oven to 450 degrees. Place the tortilla wedges on a baking sheet and sprinkle with ¼ teaspoon of the chili powder. Bake until crisp, 5 to 7 minutes.
2. Meanwhile, in a medium nonstick skillet, heat the oil over medium heat. Add the onion and garlic and cook, stirring frequently, until softened, 3 to 5 minutes. Add the cumin and remaining ½ teaspoon chili powder and cook, stirring, 1 minute.
3. Add the chicken and cook, breaking up any lumps with the back of a spoon, until no longer pink, about 5 minutes. Stir in the enchilada sauce.
4. Preheat the broiler. Spoon 1 teaspoon of the chicken filling onto each tortilla wedge. Garnish with a sliver of jalapeño pepper, then sprinkle the cheese on top. Broil 4 inches from the heat until the cheese melts, 1 to 2 minutes. Top with a small dollop of yogurt and serve hot.

Calories: 26 per nacho	Protein: 1 gm	Total Fat: 1 gm
Saturated Fat: 1 gm	Cholesterol: 4 mg	Carbohydrates: 2 gm
Sodium: 46 mg		

When buying ground chicken, make sure to read the label carefully. If it doesn't say ground from just chicken meat or skinless, the government allows skin to be ground up with the meat. When skin is one of the ingredients, the fat may double.

Chicken Pinwheels
with Basil-Ricotta Sauce

8 SERVINGS

4 skinless, boneless chicken breast halves (about 4 ounces
   each)
2 ounces goat cheese, crumbled (about ½ cup)
½ cup shredded fresh basil
1½ teaspoons sun-dried tomato bits
1 teaspoon minced shallot
½ teaspoon oregano
½ teaspoon salt
½ teaspoon freshly ground pepper
Basil-Ricotta Sauce (recipe follows)

1. Preheat the oven to 350 degrees. Coat an 8-inch square pan with
vegetable cooking spray. Place each chicken piece between 2 sheets
of wax paper and pound gently until flattened to ¼-inch thickness.
2. In a small bowl, combine the goat cheese, basil, sun-dried
tomato bits, shallot, oregano, salt and pepper. Stir to blend.
3. Spread the goat cheese mixture over each chicken piece, dividing
evenly. Roll up, jelly-roll style, and secure with wooden toothpicks.
Place seam side down in the prepared pan. Bake until the juices run
clear when the meat is pricked with a fork, 25 to 30 minutes.
Remove the picks and cut rolls into ½-inch slices. Serve with Basil-
Ricotta Sauce.

Basil-Ricotta Sauce
MAKES ABOUT 1 CUP

1 cup fresh basil leaves
¼ cup part-skim ricotta cheese
¼ cup nonfat plain yogurt
1 teaspoon minced shallot
½ teaspoon oregano

In a food processor, puree all the ingredients until smooth.

Calories: 114   Protein: 16 gm   Total Fat: 4 gm
Saturated Fat: 1 gm   Cholesterol: 42 mg   Carbohydrates: 4 gm
Sodium: 234 mg

A SUPER SOURCE OF:
Niacin   ▬▬▬▬▬▬ 33%

0%   U.S. Recommended Daily Allowance   100%

CHOICE CHICKEN SOUPS

Chicken soup—that most basic of all soups—is the cornerstone of soups of every nationality. In this chapter, diversity and international appeal is reflected in recipes like Mexican Tortilla Soup and Indian Mulligatawny Soup, while warmth and comfort emanates from recipes such as that quintessential cure-all—Mom's Chicken Noodle Soup.

Also included are recipes for two types of chicken stock—one a simple basic stock that can be used whenever chicken broth is called for in any of the recipes. The other is Chinese Chicken Stock, which gives an added dimension to any of the oriental dishes.

It's worth the minimal effort it takes to make your own stock because it can be frozen in small portions in the freezer for up to two months and used at your convenience. And they both contain no salt and very little fat. If you don't have the time to make your own stock, a good no-salt or low-sodium canned chicken broth will work well in any of the recipes. Be sure to adjust the amount of salt called for in any of the recipes if using a salted canned chicken broth.

Basic Chicken Stock

This basic chicken stock is made without salt and any fat is discarded. It can be frozen for up to 2 months in small individual portions from 2 tablespoons in individual ice cube trays up to 1-cup containers. MAKES ABOUT 3 QUARTS

3 quarts water
3 pounds chicken necks, backs, wings
1 large carrot, trimmed and halved
1 celery rib, halved
1 large onion, sliced
Bouquet garni: 1 sprig of parsley, 1 bay leaf, ¼ teaspoon thyme and 3 peppercorns tied in cheesecloth

1. In a large stockpot, heat all the ingredients to boiling. Reduce the heat and simmer, partially covered, skimming the surface occasionally, 3 to 4 hours.
2. Strain the stock through a sieve lined with a double thickness of dampened cheesecloth; discard solids. Let the stock cool to room temperature; refrigerate, covered, until cold. Remove and discard fat from the surface. The stock can be refrigerated, tightly covered, for up to 3 days, or frozen for up to 2 months. Reheat to boiling before using.

Calories: 40 per cup	Protein: 1 gm	Total Fat: 2 gm
Saturated Fat: 0 gm	Cholesterol: 0 mg	Carbohydrates: 5 gm
Sodium: 2 mg		

> *After cooking, refrigerate soups, stocks and stews and discard the fat that rises to the top and congeals on chilling.*

*M*om's Chicken Noodle Soup

8 SERVINGS (ABOUT 12 CUPS)

1 chicken (about 3 to 4 pounds), quartered
1 large onion, quartered
3 carrots, sliced
3 celery ribs with leaves
1 parsnip, sliced
4 sprigs of parsley
1½ teaspoons salt
¼ teaspoon freshly ground pepper
4 ounces egg noodles

1. Place the chicken in a large stockpot and add 2½ to 3 quarts cold water. Heat to boiling and skim off the foam. Add the onion, carrots, celery, parsnip, parsley, salt and pepper. Reduce the heat and simmer, partially covered, for 1 hour.
2. Using a slotted spoon, remove the chicken to a plate. When cool enough to handle, remove the meat from the bones. Discard the chicken skin and the bones. Shred the meat into bite-size pieces.
3. Strain the soup through a sieve and press on the solids to extract as much liquid as possible. If using immediately, skim off the fat from the broth.
4. In a large saucepan, bring the broth to a boil. Add the noodles and cook until tender, 12 to 15 minutes. Return the chicken to the soup, heat for 1 minute and serve.

Calories: 183	Protein: 23	Total Fat: 4 gm
Saturated Fat: 1 gm	Cholesterol: 80 mg	Carbohydrates: 14 gm
Sodium: 501 mg		

A SUPER SOURCE OF:

Phosphorus ▬▬▬ 21%
Vitamin A ▬▬▬▬▬▬▬▬▬▬▬▬▬ 78%
Niacin ▬▬▬▬▬▬▬ 46%

0%   U.S. Recommended Daily Allowance   100%

Grilled Corn and Chicken Soup with Roasted Pepper Puree

4 SERVINGS (ABOUT 5 CUPS)

4 ears fresh corn, husks and silk removed
2 teaspoons vegetable oil
¼ cup chopped chives
1 fresh or pickled jalapeño pepper, seeded and minced
1 teaspoon ground cumin
½ teaspoon dried thyme leaves
½ teaspoon cayenne pepper
3 cups buttermilk
2 cups diced (½-inch) cooked chicken (about ½ pound)
½ teaspoon salt
½ teaspoon freshly ground pepper
Roasted Pepper Puree (recipe follows)

1. Prepare a hot fire in a grill or preheat the broiler.
2. Grill or broil the corn, turning frequently, until lightly browned all over, 7 to 8 minutes. Let cool slightly, then cut the corn kernels from the cobs; set aside.
3. In a large saucepan, heat the oil over medium heat. Add the chives and jalapeño pepper and cook, stirring frequently, until softened, about 3 minutes. Add the cumin, thyme and cayenne and cook, stirring, 1 minute. Add the buttermilk, chicken, salt and pepper and heat over low heat just until hot.
4. Ladle the soup into bowls and top each with about 2 tablespoons Roasted Pepper Puree.

Instead of thickening soups and stews with flour and fat, puree some of the cooking vegetables and boil down the liquid to reduce to the desired consistency.

Roasted Pepper Puree

MAKES ABOUT ½ CUP

1 large red bell pepper
3 tablespoons nonfat plain yogurt
1 tablespoon chopped parsley
Pinch of salt

1. Prepare a hot fire in a grill or preheat broiler.
2. Grill or broil the pepper 4 inches from the heat, turning, until blackened all over, about 10 minutes. Let stand in a closed paper bag for about 10 minutes. Remove the stems and seeds and peel off the skin.
3. In a food processor or blender, puree the pepper, yogurt, parsley and salt until smooth. Transfer to a small bowl and let stand at room temperature for up to 2 hours before serving. Cover and refrigerate for longer storage.

Calories: 295
Saturated Fat: 3 gm
Sodium: 572 mg

Protein: 26 gm
Cholesterol: 58 mg

Total Fat: 9 gm
Carbohydrates: 29 gm

A SUPER SOURCE OF:

Calcium	—————	26%
Phosphorus	—————	38%
Vitamin A	—————	32%
Riboflavin	—————	26%
Niacin	—————	35%
Vitamin C	———————————————	79%

0%   U.S. Recommended Daily Allowance   100%

Mexican Tortilla Soup

4 SERVINGS (ABOUT 5 CUPS)

1 tablespoon vegetable oil
1 medium onion, chopped
1 garlic clove, chopped
1 jalapeño pepper, seeded and minced
¼ teaspoon cayenne pepper
2 medium tomatoes (about ¾ pound)
3 cups no-salt chicken broth
2 cups shredded cooked chicken (about ½ pound)
2 teaspoons fresh lime juice
1 teaspoon grated lime zest
½ teaspoon salt
¼ teaspoon freshly ground pepper
4 (5½-inch) stale corn tortillas, cut into ¼-inch strips
2 ounces reduced-fat Monterey Jack cheese, shredded (about ½ cup)

1. In a large nonstick skillet, heat 1 teaspoon of the oil over medium heat. Add the onion, garlic and jalapeño pepper and cook until the onion is softened, about 5 minutes. Add the cayenne and cook, stirring, 1 minute. Transfer the onion mixture to a food processor.
2. Preheat the broiler. On a foil-lined pan, broil the whole tomatoes 6 inches from the heat, turning, until charred all over, 15 to 20 minutes. Add the tomatoes to the processor and puree until smooth.
3. In a large noncorrosive saucepan, combine the tomato-onion puree and the chicken broth. Heat to boiling. Reduce the heat to low and simmer 10 minutes. Stir in the chicken, lime juice, lime zest, salt and pepper. Heat until hot.
4. Meanwhile, in a large nonstick skillet, heat the remaining 2 teaspoons oil over medium-high heat. Add the tortilla strips and cook, tossing, until browned, 8 to 10 minutes. To serve, ladle the soup into wide bowls and garnish with the tortilla strips and cheese.

Calories: 295	Protein: 25 gm	Total Fat: 13 gm
Saturated Fat: 3 gm	Cholesterol: 60 mg	Carbohydrates: 20 gm
Sodium: 513 mg		

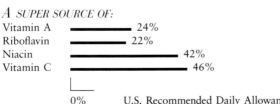

A SUPER SOURCE OF:

Vitamin A	24%
Riboflavin	22%
Niacin	42%
Vitamin C	46%

0%　　　U.S. Recommended Daily Allowance　　　100%

Creamy Carrot Soup with Chicken

This rich, smooth, low-fat soup gets its texture not from heavy cream, but from the cooked potatoes pureed with the carrots.

6 SERVINGS (ABOUT 6 CUPS)

2 teaspoons olive oil
1 large onion, chopped
1½ teaspoons ground cumin
1 pound carrots, peeled and sliced
½ pound all-purpose or russet potatoes, peeled and diced
3 cups no-salt chicken broth
1 cup low-fat milk, hot
2 cups shredded cooked chicken (about ½ pound)
1 tablespoon fresh lime juice
½ teaspoon salt
½ teaspoon ground pepper
Nonfat plain yogurt and lime slices, as garnish

1. In a large saucepan, heat the oil over medium heat. Add the onion and cook, stirring frequently, until softened, about 5 minutes. Add the cumin and cook 1 minute. Add the carrots, potatoes and chicken broth. Bring to a boil, reduce the heat to low, cover and simmer, stirring occasionally, until the vegetables are soft, 25 to 30 minutes.

2. In a food processor, puree the soup in batches until smooth. Return to the saucepan. Gradually stir in the milk and heat over low heat. Add the chicken, lime juice, salt and pepper; heat just until hot. Ladle the soup into bowls and garnish each serving with a dollop of yogurt and a lime slice.

Calories: 183	Protein: 15 gm	Total Fat: 5 gm
Saturated Fat: 1 gm	Cholesterol: 34 mg	Carbohydrates: 18 gm
Sodium: 290 mg		

A SUPER SOURCE OF:

Vitamin A ——————————————— 100%
Niacin ———— 27%
Vitamin C ———— 27%

0%   U.S. Recommended Daily Allowance   100%

Mulligatawny Soup

This spicy Indian chicken soup, which classically uses *ghee*, a kind of clarified butter, has been made healthy and low-fat with just a couple teaspoons of vegetable oil. 6 SERVINGS (ABOUT 6 CUPS)

2 teaspoons vegetable oil
1 large onion, finely chopped (about 1 cup)
1 Granny Smith apple, peeled, cored and chopped (about 1 cup)
1 carrot, peeled and finely chopped (about ⅔ cup)
1 tablespoon finely chopped fresh ginger
2 garlic cloves, minced
1 tablespoon all-purpose flour
½ teaspoon each: ground turmeric, cayenne pepper, ground ginger, ground cumin and ground coriander
4 cups no-salt chicken broth
1 cup nonfat plain yogurt
2 cups shredded cooked chicken (about ½ pound)
1 teaspoon fresh lemon juice
1 teaspoon grated lemon zest
½ teaspoon salt
½ teaspoon freshly ground pepper
2 tablespoons chopped fresh coriander or parsley

1. Heat the oil in a large saucepan over medium heat. Add the onion, apple, carrot, fresh ginger and garlic. Cook, stirring frequently, until softened, 5 to 7 minutes.
2. Add the flour, turmeric, cayenne, ground ginger, cumin and ground coriander. Cook, stirring, 2 minutes. Add the chicken broth and heat to boiling. Reduce the heat and simmer 10 minutes.
3. Pour ⅓ cup of the soup into the yogurt and stir to mix. Then spoon the yogurt mixture back into the soup. Add the shredded chicken, lemon juice, lemon zest, salt and pepper. Heat just until hot; do not boil. Ladle into soup bowls. Garnish with the fresh coriander.

Calories: 162	Protein: 15 gm	Total Fat: 6 gm
Saturated Fat: 1 gm	Cholesterol: 34 mg	Carbohydrates: 12 gm
Sodium: 285 mg		

A SUPER SOURCE OF:
Vitamin A ▬▬▬▬▬▬▬▬▬▬▬▬ 71%
Niacin ▬▬▬▬ 24%

0%   U.S. Recommended Daily Allowance   100%

Spicy Split Pea Chicken Soup

This soothing, mellow soup is given an added kick with the addition of a variety of spices. 6 SERVINGS (ABOUT 6 CUPS)

2 teaspoons vegetable oil
1 large onion, chopped (about 1 cup)
2 garlic cloves, minced
1 tablespoon chopped fresh ginger
1 teaspoon ground cumin
½ teaspoon ground ginger
¼ teaspoon ground cardamom
¼ teaspoon ground cloves
¼ teaspoon ground cinnamon
¼ teaspoon cayenne pepper
1 pound yellow or green split peas, rinsed, drained and
  picked over
6 cups no-salt chicken broth
3 cups shredded cooked chicken (about ¾ pound)
½ teaspoon salt
¼ teaspoon freshly ground pepper
1 tablespoon fresh lemon juice

1. In a large saucepan, heat the oil over medium heat. Add the onion, garlic and fresh ginger. Cook, stirring frequently, until softened, about 5 minutes. Add the cumin, ground ginger, cardamom, cloves, cinnamon and cayenne. Cook, stirring, 1 to 2 minutes.
2. Add the split peas and cook, stirring to coat, 1 minute. Add the chicken broth and heat to boiling. Reduce the heat, cover and simmer until the split peas are tender, 1½ to 2 hours.
3. Add the chicken, salt and pepper and cook just until heated through. Stir in the lemon juice. Add more chicken broth or water, if needed, to make a soupy consistency.

Calories: 423	Protein: 38 gm	Total Fat: 8 gm
Saturated Fat: 2 gm	Cholesterol: 50 mg	Carbohydrates: 50 gm
Sodium: 297 mg		

A SUPER SOURCE OF:

Phosphorus	━━━━━━━━	40%
Iron	━━━━━	29%
Thiamin	━━━━━━━━	41%
Niacin	━━━━━━━━━	45%

0%   U.S. Recommended Daily Allowance   100%

Smoked Chicken-Mushroom Soup

Leftover shredded cooked chicken is equally delicious in this soup. 4 SERVINGS

1 tablespoon olive oil
½ cup chopped shallots or onion
1 pound fresh mushrooms, coarsely chopped
1 tablespoon all-purpose flour
4 cups no-salt chicken broth
¾ pound all-purpose potatoes, peeled and diced
1 bay leaf
4 ounces smoked chicken, shredded
2 teaspoons fresh lemon juice
½ teaspoon dried thyme leaves
½ teaspoon salt
¼ teaspoon freshly ground pepper
2 tablespoons chopped parsley

1. In a large saucepan, heat the oil over medium heat. Add the shallots and cook, stirring constantly, until softened, 3 to 5 minutes. Add the mushrooms and cook, stirring frequently, 7 to 8 minutes. Add the flour and cook, stirring, 2 to 3 minutes. Add the chicken broth, potatoes and bay leaf and heat to boiling. Reduce the heat and simmer until the potatoes are tender, 25 to 30 minutes; discard the bay leaf.
2. In a food processor, puree the soup in batches until smooth.
3. Return the soup to the saucepan. Add the chicken, lemon juice, thyme, salt and pepper. Heat just until hot. Ladle into soup bowls. Garnish with the parsley.

Calories: 228	Protein: 15 gm	Total Fat: 8 gm
Saturated Fat: 2 gm	Cholesterol: 25 mg	Carbohydrates: 26 gm
Sodium: 614 mg		

A SUPER SOURCE OF:

Phosphorus	23%
Iron	22%
Riboflavin	38%
Niacin	50%
Vitamin C	40%

0%   U.S. Recommended Daily Allowance   100%

Chicken Vegetable Soup

6 SERVINGS (ABOUT 8 CUPS)

2 teaspoons vegetable oil
2 medium onions, chopped (about 1½ cups)
2 medium leeks (white part only), thinly sliced
1 large garlic clove, chopped
2 medium turnips, peeled and cut into ½-inch dice
½ pound all-purpose potatoes, peeled and cut into ½-inch dice
½ pound fresh mushrooms, thickly sliced
4 carrots, cut into ½-inch slices
5 cups no-salt chicken broth
⅓ cup toasted barley shapes or pastina
6 ounces fresh spinach, rinsed well, leaves torn into 2-inch pieces
1 teaspoon salt
½ teaspoon freshly ground pepper
3 cups diced cooked chicken (about ¾ pound)
3 tablespoons chopped parsley
Grated Parmesan cheese (optional)

1. In a large saucepan, heat the oil over medium heat. Add the onions, leeks and garlic. Cook, stirring frequently, until softened, about 5 minutes. Add the turnips, potatoes, mushrooms and carrots. Cook, stirring frequently, 3 minutes. Add the chicken broth and heat to boiling. Add the barley shapes, reduce the heat and simmer, covered, until the vegetables are crisp-tender, 8 to 10 minutes.

2. Add the spinach, salt and pepper. Cover and cook until the vegetables are tender, about 5 minutes. Add the chicken and heat through.

3. Ladle the soup into warmed soup bowls. Garnish with the parsley. Serve with Parmesan cheese, if desired.

Calories: 276	Protein: 23 gm	Total Fat: 8 gm
Saturated Fat: 2 gm	Cholesterol: 58 mg	Carbohydrates: 29 gm
Sodium: 535 mg		

A SUPER SOURCE OF:

Phosphorus	———— 25%	
Iron	———— 23%	
Vitamin A	———————————————————— 100%	
Riboflavin	———— 26%	
Niacin	———————— 50%	
Vitamin C	——————————— 59%	

0%   U.S. Recommended Daily Allowance   100%

SENSIBLE SANDWICHES

There's more to fillings to chicken sandwiches than chicken salad and more than just bread that encloses those fillings.

Sandwiches run the gamut from hot to cold, from hearty hero to tiny tea sandwich, from closed to open-faced. The variation is limitless, even when the main component each time is chicken, because chicken is as versatile as the sandwiches themselves.

While sandwiches do have a reputation for being high in calories and fat and low in nutritional value, this is due to fillings that consist of meats and cheeses high in fat, spreads such as mayonnaise, butter and cream cheese, and cottony-textured white bread.

Taking a cue from the title, this chapter proves that sensible sandwiches can be delicious as well as wholesome and nutritious. They can have interesting, inventive, flavorful fillings — and still be good for you.

Take your pick from this diverse array of healthful sandwiches and see if they pass muster — or is it mustard?

New Wave Reuben on Rye

4 SERVINGS

4 skinless, boneless chicken breast halves (4 ounces each)
Russian Slaw (recipe follows)
8 slices of rye bread
4 thin slices of Canadian bacon (2 ounces)
4 slices of red onion
4 thin slices of reduced-fat Swiss cheese (2 ounces)

1. Place each piece of chicken between 2 pieces of plastic wrap. Pound gently to flatten each piece to an even ¼-inch thickness.
2. Coat a large nonstick skillet with vegetable cooking spray and heat over medium heat. Add the chicken and cook, turning once, until the cutlets are browned, about 6 minutes.
3. Spoon the slaw onto 4 of the bread slices. Place a chicken cutlet, a slice of Canadian bacon, red onion and then cheese on top of the slaw. Top with the remaining bread slices.
4. Coat the same skillet again with vegetable cooking spray and heat over medium-high heat. Grill the sandwiches, turning once, until browned, 5 to 6 minutes.

Russian Slaw

MAKES ABOUT 2 CUPS

¼ cup nonfat plain yogurt
1 tablespoon ketchup
1 tablespoon sweet pickle relish
1 tablespoon prepared white horseradish
½ teaspoon Worcestershire sauce
2 cups shredded cabbage
1 tablespoon caraway seeds

In a medium bowl, combine the yogurt, ketchup, relish, horseradish and Worcestershire sauce. Stir to blend well. Add the cabbage and caraway seeds and toss to mix.

Calories: 398	Protein: 45 gm	Total Fat: 9 gm
Saturated Fat: 4 gm	Cholesterol: 94 mg	Carbohydrates: 35 gm
Sodium: 697 mg		

A SUPER SOURCE OF:

Calcium	▬▬▬▬▬▬	46%
Niacin	▬▬▬▬▬▬▬▬▬	76%
Vitamin C	▬▬▬▬	37%

0%   U.S. Recommended Daily Allowance   100%

Smoked Chicken and Shrimp Salad Sandwich with Watercress Dressing

These sandwiches can also be served open-faced. 4 SERVINGS

6 ounces cooked shelled and deveined medium shrimp
Watercress Dressing (recipe follows)
8 thin slices of whole grain bread
12 to 16 watercress sprigs
16 thin slices of peeled, seeded cucumber
4 ounces smoked chicken, thinly sliced

1. Combine the shrimp and half the Watercress Dressing in a medium bowl; stir until coated.
2. Spread the remaining dressing over 4 of the bread slices. Place the watercress sprigs, cucumber, shrimp salad and smoked chicken on top, dividing evenly. Top with the remaining bread slices.

Watercress Dressing

MAKES ABOUT ½ CUP

½ cup nonfat plain yogurt
2 tablespoons chopped watercress leaves
2 teaspoons Dijon mustard
2 teaspoons fresh lemon juice
¼ teaspoon freshly ground pepper

In a small bowl, combine all the ingredients; stir until blended.

Calories: 188	Protein: 22 gm	Total Fat: 4 gm
Saturated Fat: 1 gm	Cholesterol: 110 mg	Carbohydrates: 18 gm
Sodium: 617 mg		

A SUPER SOURCE OF:
Phosphorus ━━━━━ 23%
Niacin ━━━━━ 23%

0%   U.S. Recommended Daily Allowance   100%

Chicken and Roasted Pepper Heros

4 SERVINGS

2 tablespoons prepared pesto
2 tablespoons nonfat plain yogurt
1 tablespoon minced sun-dried tomato bits
4 skinless, boneless chicken breast halves (4 ounces each)
4 Italian hero rolls
1 small bunch of arugula or watercress, trimmed
1 jar (7 ounces) roasted red peppers, rinsed, drained and
   quartered
12 romaine lettuce leaves

1. In a small bowl, combine the pesto, yogurt and sun-dried tomatoes; mix until blended.
2. Coat a large nonstick skillet with vegetable cooking spray and heat over medium-high heat. Add the chicken and cook, turning once, until browned, 6 to 8 minutes.
3. Spread the sun-dried pesto on the bottom half of each roll. Layer the arugula, chicken, peppers and romaine lettuce on top of the pesto. Place the top half of each roll on the lettuce.

Calories: 439   Protein: 37 gm   Total Fat: 8 gm
Saturated Fat: 2 gm   Cholesterol: 70 mg   Carbohydrates: 53 gm
Sodium: 646 mg

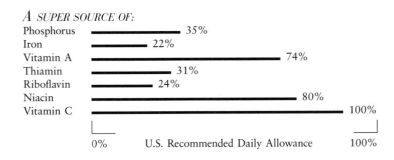

A SUPER SOURCE OF:

Phosphorus	35%
Iron	22%
Vitamin A	74%
Thiamin	31%
Riboflavin	24%
Niacin	80%
Vitamin C	100%

0%   U.S. Recommended Daily Allowance   100%

The National Research Council suggests that you eat at least five servings of fruit and vegetables and at least six servings of breads, cereals and legumes a day.

Southwestern Chicken Cheeseburger

4 SERVINGS

1 pound ground chicken
½ cup shredded zucchini
2 tablespoons chopped parsley
1 tablespoon minced and seeded pickled jalapeño pepper
½ teaspoon salt
¼ teaspoon freshly ground pepper
10 cherry tomatoes, halved
1 red or yellow bell pepper, finely diced
1 scallion, chopped
2 teaspoons fresh lime juice
2 ounces reduced-fat Monterey Jack cheese, thinly sliced
4 hamburger rolls, halved and toasted

1. In a large bowl, combine the chicken, zucchini, parsley, jalapeño pepper, salt and pepper. Stir until well blended. Shape into 4 patties about ½ inch thick.

2. Preheat the broiler. Broil the patties 4 inches from the heat, turning once, until cooked through and no longer pink, 13 to 15 minutes.

3. Meanwhile, in a small bowl, combine the tomatoes, bell pepper, scallion and lime juice. Stir to blend.

4. Place the cheese on top of the burgers and broil just until melted, about 1 minute.

5. Place a cheeseburger on bottom of each roll. Top with the tomato mixture.

Calories: 349	Protein: 28 gm	Total Fat: 15 gm
Saturated Fat: 5 gm	Cholesterol: 107 mg	Carbohydrates: 24 gm
Sodium: 693 mg		

A SUPER SOURCE OF:

Iron	━━━ 21%	
Vitamin A	━━━━━ 41%	
Riboflavin	━━━ 24%	
Niacin	━━━━ 32%	
Vitamin C	━━━━━━━━━━━ 81%	

0%   U.S. Recommended Daily Allowance   100%

*I*talian Chicken Cheeseburger

The flavor of this burger is heightened by a topping of sautéed onions, peppers and mushrooms.   4 SERVINGS

1 pound ground chicken
½ cup shredded zucchini
1 teaspoon oregano
½ teaspoon salt
¼ teaspoon freshly ground pepper
2 teaspoons olive oil
1 medium onion, thinly sliced
1 green bell pepper, cut into ¼-inch slices
2 ounces mushrooms, thinly sliced (about ½ cup)
2 ounces part-skim mozzarella cheese, thinly sliced
4 hamburger rolls, halved and toasted

1. In a large bowl, combine the ground chicken, zucchini, oregano, salt and pepper. Mix until well blended. Shape into 4 patties about ½ inch thick.
2. Preheat the broiler. Broil the patties 4 inches from the heat, turning once, until cooked through and no longer pink, 13 to 15 minutes.
3. Meanwhile, in a large nonstick skillet, heat the olive oil over medium heat. Add the onion and bell pepper and cook, stirring, until crisp-tender, about 3 minutes. Add the mushrooms and cook until softened, 2 to 3 minutes; remove from the heat.
4. Place a slice of cheese on top of each burger and broil just until melted, about 1 minute.
5. Place a cheeseburger on the bottom half of each roll. Top with the onion-pepper mixture.

Calories: 369	Protein: 28 gm	Total Fat: 17 gm
Saturated Fat: 5 gm	Cholesterol: 105 mg	Carbohydrates: 25 gm
Sodium: 636 mg		

A SUPER SOURCE OF:

Phosphorus	━━━━	26%
Iron	━━━	21%
Riboflavin	━━━━	26%
Niacin	━━━━━	34%
Vitamin C	━━━━━━━━	51%

0%   U.S. Recommended Daily Allowance   100%

Middle Eastern Meatballs in Whole Wheat Pitas

The secret to keeping these chicken meatballs moist is the shredded zucchini. 4 SERVINGS

8 ounces zucchini
¾ pound ground chicken
¼ cup dry bread crumbs
¼ cup finely chopped onion
¼ cup chopped fresh mint
1 teaspoon ground cumin
¼ teaspoon salt
¼ teaspoon freshly ground pepper
1 large egg
4 whole wheat pita breads, warmed
Mint Sauce (recipe follows)

1. Thinly slice half of the zucchini and set aside. Shred the remaining zucchini. In a large bowl, combine the ground chicken, shredded zucchini, bread crumbs, onion, mint, cumin, salt, pepper and egg. Stir until well blended. Shape into 1-inch balls.
2. Coat a large nonstick skillet with vegetable cooking spray and heat over medium heat. Add the sliced zucchini and cook, stirring frequently, until lightly browned, 4 to 5 minutes. Transfer to a plate.
3. Coat the same skillet with vegetable cooking spray and heat over medium heat. Add the meatballs in a single layer and cook, shaking the pan frequently, until browned and cooked through, 13 to 15 minutes.
4. Spoon the meatballs into the pitas, dividing evenly. Top with the sautéed sliced zucchini and the mint sauce.

*M*int *Sauce*

MAKES ABOUT 1 CUP

1 cup nonfat plain yogurt
¼ cup peeled, seeded and diced cucumber
¼ cup diced fresh tomato
2 tablespoons chopped fresh mint
¼ teaspoon freshly ground pepper
¼ teaspoon cayenne

In a small bowl, combine all the ingredients until well blended.

Calories: 393	Protein: 28 gm	Total Fat: 10 gm
Saturated Fat: 2 gm	Cholesterol: 125 mg	Carbohydrates: 48 gm
Sodium: 678 mg		

A SUPER SOURCE OF:

Phosphorus ▬▬▬▬▬▬▬ 37%
Iron ▬▬▬▬▬ 26%
Thiamin ▬▬▬▬▬ 28%
Riboflavin ▬▬▬▬▬▬ 35%
Niacin ▬▬▬▬▬▬ 34%
Vitamin C ▬▬▬▬ 22%

0%   U.S. Recommended Daily Allowance   100%

Ask your butcher to grind skinless chicken for you, even though it will cost a little more than the prepackaged ground chicken. At least you know exactly what you're getting.

California Chicken Cheeseburger

The classic burger and so-o California—made with ground chicken instead of beef. 4 SERVINGS

1 pound ground chicken
½ cup shredded zucchini
3 tablespoons chopped parsley
½ teaspoon salt
¼ teaspoon freshly ground pepper
2 ounces reduced-fat Monterey Jack cheese, thinly sliced
¼ cup nonfat plain yogurt
4 leaves of curly leaf lettuce
4 whole wheat hamburger rolls, halved and toasted
4 slices of red onion
4 slices of tomato
¼ cup shredded peeled carrot
¼ cup radish or alfalfa sprouts

1. In a large bowl, combine the ground chicken, zucchini, 2 tablespoons of the parsley, salt and pepper. Mix until well blended. Shape into 4 patties about ½ inch thick.

2. Preheat the broiler. Broil 4 inches from the heat, turning once, until cooked through and no longer pink, 13 to 15 minutes. Top with the cheese and broil just until melted, about 1 minute.

3. Meanwhile, in a small bowl, combine the yogurt and remaining 1 tablespoon chopped parsley.

4. Place a lettuce leaf on the bottom half of each roll. Place a cheeseburger on the lettuce and add a slice of red onion, tomato, and 1 tablespoon shredded carrot and radish sprouts. Top with a dollop of the yogurt mixture.

Calories: 356	Protein: 28 gm	Total Fat: 15 gm
Saturated Fat: 5 gm	Cholesterol: 107 mg	Carbohydrates: 25 gm
Sodium: 674 mg		

A SUPER SOURCE OF:

Calcium	———— 23%	
Phosphorus	——— 20%	
Iron	——— 20%	
Vitamin A	————————— 55%	
Riboflavin	———— 25%	
Niacin	———— 31%	
Vitamin C	——— 21%	

0%   U.S. Recommended Daily Allowance   100%

SENSATIONAL SALADS

Salads can play many roles in the course of a meal: at the beginning it acts to stimulate one's appetite; as a side dish, it counterbalances or lightens the main meal; after the main course, it cleanses the palate before dessert. The salads in this chapter, though, are on center stage—as the main event.

When composing a salad, always pick the freshest ingredients from the market and choose what's in season. Although salads connote healthy eating, many ingredients and the dressing that binds them together can quickly turn into a caloric nightmare. Stay away from high-fat cheeses, marinated jarred vegetables and salty toppings. Opt instead for chicken paired with grains as in the Chicken Couscous Salad or Wild Rice Chicken Salad with Buttermilk Chive Dressing. Use cheese sparingly, and try a low-fat one, such as in the Chicken Salad Tostadas. Toasted nuts add a crunchy flavorful dimension to the Double Pear Chicken Salad, but are used in small amounts. Switch from high-fat dressings made with mayonnaise, sour cream and lots of oil to buttermilk or yogurt-based dressings. Reverse the ratios in oil-based acid dressings: increase the acid and lower the oil.

These salads represent a multitude of nationalities—from Mexican Chicken Salad Tostadas, Thai Chicken Salad and Chinese Mandarin Chicken Salad to the classic American Cobb Salad—and they are beautifully presented, whether tossed, layered or arranged. They're a great way for using leftover chicken, but if you don't have any on hand, it takes only a few minutes to poach chicken breasts, cool, then shred or dice. Cooked chicken can also be purchased from your local supermarket or deli.

Because chicken is so adaptable, the creation of any number of salads is possible. Try some of the delectable ideas in this chapter and see if you're not inspired to come up with your own house salads.

*C*obb Salad

The original Brown Derby restaurant in Los Angeles is where the Cobb salad was reportedly created. To make it healthier, I've substituted thin strips of low-fat turkey ham for bacon and hard-cooked egg whites for egg yolks. 4 SERVINGS

1 pound boneless, skinless chicken breast halves
2 tablespoons white wine vinegar
2 teaspoons vegetable oil
2 ounces blue cheese, crumbled (about ½ cup)
½ teaspoon salt
½ teaspoon freshly ground pepper
8 cups shredded romaine or iceberg lettuce
4 hard-cooked egg whites
½ firm ripe avocado, peeled, pitted and cut into thin strips
1 pound fresh ripe tomatoes, cut into ½-inch dice (about 2 cups)
8 radishes, trimmed and thinly sliced
2 ounces low-fat turkey ham, cut into thin strips
½ cup diced red onion

1. Place the chicken in a large skillet. Add water to cover and heat to a simmer. Reduce the heat to low and poach, uncovered, until the chicken is white throughout, 7 to 8 minutes. Remove the chicken, cover loosely and let stand until cool enough to handle. Cut the chicken into 1-inch pieces.
2. In a small bowl, whisk together the wine vinegar, oil, blue cheese, salt and pepper.
3. Place the lettuce in a large bowl. Arrange the chicken, egg whites, avocado, tomatoes, radishes, turkey ham and onion on top. Just before serving, drizzle the dressing over the salad and toss.

Calories: 334	Protein: 39 mg	Total Fat: 14 gm
Saturated Fat: 5 gm	Cholesterol: 81 mg	Carbohydrates: 12 gm
Sodium: 748 mg		

A SUPER SOURCE OF:

Phosphorus	33%
Vitamin A	89%
Riboflavin	31%
Niacin	51%
Vitamin C	88%

0%   U.S. Recommended Daily Allowance   100%

*W*ild Rice Chicken Salad with Buttermilk Chive Dressing

4 SERVINGS

6 ounces wild rice (about 1 cup)
½ pound skinless, boneless chicken breast halves
4 cups shredded romaine lettuce
1 cup red seedless grapes, halved
8 dried peach halves, quartered
6 radishes, finely diced (about ¾ cup)
½ cup buttermilk
¼ cup chopped fresh chives
2 tablespoons fresh lemon juice
½ teaspoon salt
½ teaspoon freshly ground pepper

1. In a large saucepan, heat 4 cups water to boiling over high heat. Add the rice and cook according to package directions.
2. Meanwhile, place the chicken in a large skillet. Add water to cover and heat to a simmer. Reduce the heat to low and poach, uncovered, until the chicken is white throughout, 7 to 8 minutes. Remove the chicken, cover loosely and let stand until cool enough to handle. Cut the chicken into 1-inch dice.
3. In a large bowl, combine the chicken, wild rice, lettuce, grapes, dried peaches and radishes.
4. In a small bowl, combine the buttermilk, chives, lemon juice, salt and pepper; blend well. Pour over the rice salad and toss to combine. Serve warm or at room temperature.

Calories: 325	Protein: 23 gm	Total Fat: 3 gm
Saturated Fat: 1 gm	Cholesterol: 36 mg	Carbohydrates: 56 gm
Sodium: 349 mg		

A SUPER SOURCE OF:

Phosphorus	———— 35%
Vitamin A	————— 45%
Niacin	———— 41%
Vitamin C	———— 44%

0%   U.S. Recommended Daily Allowance   100%

Eating foods high in fiber (wheat bran, whole grains, oats, beans, carrots, apples and oranges) fills you up and leaves less room for high-fat foods.

*M*editerranean Chicken Potato Salad

4 SERVINGS

1 pound small red potatoes, quartered
1 pound skinless, boneless chicken breast halves
2 ounces slivered almonds
2 tablespoons red wine vinegar
1 tablespoon olive oil
2 tablespoons chopped fresh mint, or 1 teaspoon dried, crumbled
½ teaspoon salt
½ teaspoon freshly ground pepper
1 medium cucumber, peeled, seeded and diced (about ¾ cup)
1 medium red bell pepper, diced (about ¾ cup)
2 scallions, thinly sliced (about ⅓ cup)
10 Calamata olives, halved and pitted
3 ounces feta cheese, crumbled (about ¾ cup)

1. Place potatoes in a medium saucepan. Add water to cover and heat to boiling. Cook until potatoes are tender, about 20 minutes; drain.
2. Meanwhile place the chicken in a large skillet. Add water to cover and heat to a simmer. Reduce the heat to low and poach, uncovered, until the chicken is white throughout, 7 to 8 minutes. Remove the chicken, cover loosely and let stand until cool enough to handle. Cut the chicken into 1-inch pieces.
3. In a small skillet, toast the almonds over medium heat, shaking the pan frequently, until browned, about 5 minutes; set aside.
4. In a large bowl, whisk together the vinegar, olive oil, mint, salt and pepper. Add the potatoes, chicken, cucumber, bell pepper, scallions, olives, cheese and toasted almonds; toss to combine. Serve warm or at room temperature.

Calories: 433	Protein: 35 gm	Total Fat: 20 gm
Saturated Fat: 5 gm	Cholesterol: 90 mg	Carbohydrates: 27 gm
Sodium: 779 mg		

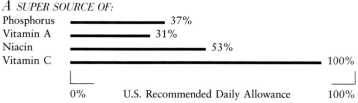

A SUPER SOURCE OF:

Phosphorus ━━━━━━━━━ 37%
Vitamin A ━━━━━━━ 31%
Niacin ━━━━━━━━━━━ 53%
Vitamin C ━━━━━━━━━━━━━━━━━━━━━━━ 100%

0%   U.S. Recommended Daily Allowance   100%

Double Pear Chicken Salad

4 SERVINGS

1 pound skinless, boneless chicken breast halves
2 ounces walnuts (about ½ cup)
2 tablespoons red wine vinegar
2 teaspoons extra-virgin olive oil
2 teaspoons Dijon mustard
½ teaspoon salt
½ teaspoon freshly ground pepper
1 head chicory lettuce, torn into pieces
1 bunch of watercress, trimmed
2 firm ripe pears, peeled and thinly sliced
4 dried pear halves, cut in half
2 ounces goat cheese, cut into 8 thin slices

1. Place the chicken in a large skillet. Add water to cover and heat to a simmer. Reduce the heat to low and poach, uncovered, until the chicken is white throughout, 7 to 8 minutes. Remove the chicken, cover loosely and let stand until cool enough to handle. Cut the chicken into 1-inch pieces.
2. In a small skillet, toast the walnuts over medium heat, shaking pan frequently, until browned, about 5 minutes; set aside.
3. In a small bowl, whisk together the vinegar, oil, mustard, salt and pepper.
4. In a large bowl, combine the lettuce, watercress, chicken, fresh and dried pears and walnuts. Pour on the vinaigrette and toss to coat.
5. Divide the salad among 4 serving plates. Arrange slices of goat cheese on top of each salad.

Calories: 432	Protein: 35 gm	Total Fat: 19 gm
Saturated Fat: 2 gm	Cholesterol: 84 mg	Carbohydrates: 35 gm
Sodium: 565 mg		

A SUPER SOURCE OF:

Calcium	23%
Phosphorus	30%
Vitamin A	100%
Riboflavin	20%
Niacin	44%
Vitamin C	84%

0%   U.S. Recommended Daily Allowance   100%

Chicken and Black-Eyed Pea Salad

Part of the legume family, black-eyed peas are low in calories (about 105 per ½ cup cooked peas), have no fat and are an excellent source of soluble fiber. 4 SERVINGS

1 ounce slivered almonds
½ pound skinless, boneless chicken breast halves
1 can (16 ounces) black-eyed peas, rinsed and drained, or
  1 package (10 ounces) frozen, thawed
½ pound summer squash, quartered lengthwise and sliced
  (about 2 cups)
2 carrots, peeled and sliced (about 1 cup)
1 red bell pepper, cut into ½-inch dice (about 1 cup)
1 bunch of watercress, trimmed
2 scallions, sliced
¼ cup chopped parsley
2 tablespoons fresh lemon juice
2 teaspoons olive oil
1 teaspoon grainy mustard
¾ teaspoon salt
½ teaspoon freshly ground pepper

1. In a small skillet, toast the almonds over medium heat, shaking the pan frequently, until browned, about 5 minutes; set aside.
2. Place the chicken in a large skillet. Add water to cover and heat to a simmer. Reduce the heat to low and poach, uncovered, until chicken is white throughout, 7 to 9 minutes. Remove the chicken, cover loosely and let stand until cool enough to handle. Cut the chicken into ½-inch dice.
3. In a large bowl, combine the chicken, black-eyed peas, squash, carrots, bell pepper, watercress, scallions, parsley and almonds. Toss to mix.
4. In a small bowl, whisk together the lemon juice, olive oil, mustard, salt and pepper. Pour the dressing over the chicken salad and toss to coat. Serve at room temperature.

Calories: 258	Protein: 22 gm	Total Fat: 8 gm
Saturated Fat: 1 gm	Cholesterol: 35 mg	Carbohydrates: 26 gm
Sodium: 724 mg		

A SUPER SOURCE OF:

Phosphorus	▬▬▬▬ 26%	
Vitamin A	▬▬▬▬▬▬▬▬▬▬▬▬▬▬▬	100%
Niacin	▬▬▬▬ 26%	
Vitamin C	▬▬▬▬▬▬▬▬▬▬▬▬▬▬▬	100%

0%   U.S. Recommended Daily Allowance   100%

Chicken Salad Tostadas

4 SERVINGS

½ pound skinless, boneless chicken breast halves
4 (5½-inch) corn tortillas
1 cup shredded iceberg lettuce
½ cup corn kernels
½ cup canned black beans, rinsed and drained
¼ cup thinly sliced jicama or radish
¼ cup diced fresh tomato
2 tablespoons chopped fresh coriander or parsley
1 tablespoon fresh lime juice
2 teaspoons vegetable oil
½ teaspoon salt
¼ teaspoon freshly ground pepper
¼ cup nonfat plain yogurt
¼ cup shredded reduced-fat Monterey Jack cheese
2 tablespoons unsalted shelled pumpkin seeds (pepitas)

1. Place the chicken in a large skillet. Add water to cover and heat to a simmer. Reduce heat to low and poach, uncovered, until the chicken is white throughout, 7 to 9 minutes. Remove the chicken, cover loosely and let stand until cool enough to handle. Cut the chicken into thin strips; set aside.
2. Coat a medium nonstick skillet with vegetable cooking spray and heat over medium-high heat. Add the tortillas, one at a time, and cook, turning once, until crisp, 3 to 4 minutes.
3. In a large bowl, combine the lettuce, chicken, corn, black beans, jicama and tomato. Toss to mix.
4. In a small bowl, whisk together the coriander, lime juice, oil, salt and pepper. Pour over the chicken mixture and toss to combine. Spoon the salad onto the tortillas, dividing evenly. Top each with 1 tablespoon yogurt, 1 tablespoon cheese and ½ tablespoon pumpkin seeds.

Calories: 246	Protein: 21 gm	Total Fat: 7 gm
Saturated Fat: 2 gm	Cholesterol: 40 mg	Carbohydrates: 26 gm
Sodium: 532 mg		

A SUPER SOURCE OF:
Phosphorus ▬▬▬ 21%
Vitamin C ▬▬▬▬ 30%

⌞___   ___⌟
0%   U.S. Recommended Daily Allowance   100%

Thai Chicken Salad

Traditionally made with beef, this salad is equally good with chicken. 4 SERVINGS

1 pound skinless, boneless chicken breast halves
1 head of romaine lettuce, shredded (8 cups)
1 cup fresh mint leaves
1 small red onion, thinly sliced
8 radishes, thinly sliced
1 cucumber, peeled, seeded and cut into 3 × ½-inch strips
¼ cup fresh lime juice
2 tablespoons vegetable oil
2 tablespoons Thai fish sauce (nam pla)*
2 teaspoons grated fresh ginger
1 teaspoon sugar
1 hot chili pepper, seeded and finely minced, or ½ teaspoon crushed hot pepper flakes
2 tablespoons chopped unsalted roasted peanuts

1. Place the chicken in a large skillet. Add water to cover and heat to a simmer. Reduce the heat to low and poach, uncovered, until the chicken is white throughout, 7 to 9 minutes. Remove the chicken, cover loosely and let stand until cool enough to handle. Cut the chicken into thin strips.
2. In a large bowl, combine the chicken, lettuce, mint, red onion, radishes and cucumber. Toss to mix.
3. In a small bowl, whisk together the lime juice, oil, fish sauce, ginger, sugar and chili pepper. Pour over the salad and toss to coat. Divide the salad among 4 serving plates. Garnish with chopped peanuts.

Calories: 287	Protein: 32 gm	Total Fat: 13 gm
Saturated Fat: 2 gm	Cholesterol: 71 mg	Carbohydrates: 11 gm
Sodium: 73 mg		

A SUPER SOURCE OF:

Phosphorus	▬▬▬ 22%
Vitamin A	▬▬▬▬▬▬▬▬▬ 69%
Niacin	▬▬▬▬▬▬ 46%
Vitamin C	▬▬▬▬▬▬▬▬▬▬▬ 89%

0%   U.S. Recommended Daily Allowance   100%

*Nam pla, a fermented fish sauce of Thai origin (also called nuoc nam), is available in Oriental groceries and in the Asian section of some supermarkets. If unavailable, mash 1 anchovy fillet in 2 teaspoons low-sodium soy sauce and 1 teaspoon water.

Chicken Couscous Salad

4 SERVINGS

3/4 pound skinless, boneless chicken breast halves
1/2 teaspoon salt
1 cup couscous
1 carrot, finely diced (about 1/2 cup)
1/2 cup currants
2 scallions, thinly sliced
2 ounces slivered almonds, toasted
2 tablespoons olive oil
1/4 cup fresh lemon juice
1 teaspoon ground cumin
1/2 teaspoon grated lemon zest
1/2 teaspoon ground turmeric
1/4 teaspoon freshly ground black pepper
1/4 teaspoon cayenne pepper
Romaine lettuce leaves

1. Place the chicken in a large skillet. Add water to cover and heat to a simmer. Reduce the heat to low and poach, uncovered, until the chicken is white throughout, 7 to 9 minutes. Remove the chicken, cover loosely and let stand until cool enough to handle. Cut into thin strips.

2. Meanwhile, in a medium saucepan, heat 1 1/2 cups water and the salt to boiling. Stir in the couscous, cover and remove from the heat. Let stand until all the liquid is absorbed, about 5 minutes.

3. In a large bowl, combine the chicken, couscous, carrot, currants, scallions and toasted almonds.

4. In a small bowl, whisk together the olive oil, lemon juice, cumin, lemon zest, turmeric, black pepper and cayenne. Pour over the chicken couscous salad and toss to coat.

5. Line 4 serving plates with romaine lettuce leaves. Spoon the chicken couscous salad on top. Serve warm or at room temperature.

Calories: 487	Protein: 30 gm	Total Fat: 17 gm
Saturated Fat: 2 gm	Cholesterol: 53 mg	Carbohydrates: 56 gm
Sodium: 331 mg		

A SUPER SOURCE OF:

Phosphorus   ▬▬▬▬▬ 30%
Vitamin A   ▬▬▬▬▬▬▬▬▬▬▬▬▬▬▬▬ 87%
Niacin   ▬▬▬▬▬▬▬ 42%
Vitamin C   ▬▬▬▬ 22%

0%   U.S. Recommended Daily Allowance   100%

*M*andarin Chicken Salad

4 SERVINGS

1 pound boneless, skinless chicken breast halves
½ teaspoon Asian sesame oil
1 garlic clove, crushed
2 scallions, sliced
2 ounces snow peas, trimmed (about ½ cup)
½ pound fresh mushrooms, preferably shiitake, stemmed
  and quartered
1 can (11 ounces) mandarin oranges in light syrup, drained
6 radishes, quartered
2 ounces unsalted roasted cashews (½ cup)
¼ cup chopped parsley
2 tablespoons reduced-sodium soy sauce or tamari
2 tablespoons rice wine vinegar
2 teaspoons vegetable oil
½ teaspoon cayenne pepper
12 romaine lettuce leaves

1. Place the chicken in a large skillet. Add water to cover and heat
to a simmer. Reduce the heat to low and poach, uncovered, until
the chicken is white throughout, 7 to 9 minutes. Remove the
chicken, cover loosely and let stand until cool enough to handle.
Cut the chicken into 1-inch dice. In a large bowl, toss the chicken
with the sesame oil.
2. Coat a large nonstick skillet or wok with vegetable cooking
spray and heat over medium-high heat. Add the garlic, scallions and
snow peas and cook, stirring constantly, 1 minute. Transfer to the
bowl with the chicken. Add the mushrooms and cook, stirring
frequently, until softened, 5 to 7 minutes. Add to the bowl with the
chicken. Add the mandarin oranges, radishes, cashews and parsley.
Toss to mix.
3. In a small bowl, whisk together the soy sauce, vinegar, oil and
cayenne. Pour over the chicken salad and toss to coat.

4. Line 4 serving plates with the lettuce leaves. Spoon the salad on top.

Calories: 332   Protein: 32 gm   Total Fat: 13 gm
Saturated Fat: 2 gm   Cholesterol: 71 mg   Carbohydrates: 24 gm
Sodium: 375 mg

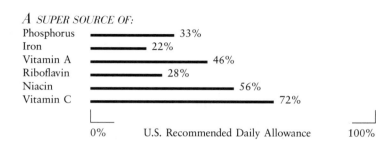

A SUPER SOURCE OF:

Phosphorus ━━━━━━━━ 33%
Iron ━━━━━ 22%
Vitamin A ━━━━━━━━━━ 46%
Riboflavin ━━━━━━ 28%
Niacin ━━━━━━━━━━━━ 56%
Vitamin C ━━━━━━━━━━━━━━ 72%

⌞   ⌟
0%   U.S. Recommended Daily Allowance   100%

Salmonella, an intestinal bacteria, is usually transmitted before poultry has been cooked. To reduce this risk, consumers should follow these few steps.
1. Rinse chicken thoroughly before cooking.
2. Use plastic cutting boards instead of wood, where deep cracks permit bacteria to flourish.
3. Wash hands, cutting utensils and cutting boards with soap and hot water immediately after working with poultry.
4. Use clean knives and cutting boards to prepare other ingredients.
5. Cook chicken thoroughly, because cooking kills salmonella and other bacteria.

Cut calories in dressings and marinades by using fruit juices, vinegars and chicken broth and reverse the ratio of oil and acid.

Chicken Corn Salad

4 SERVINGS

*3 medium bell peppers, preferably 1 red, 1 yellow and 1
  green*
1¼ pounds skinless, boneless chicken breast halves
*1½ cups fresh corn kernels (from about 3 ears), or canned
  or frozen*
1 scallion, sliced
2 tablespoons cider vinegar
1 tablespoon olive oil
1 tablespoon chopped parsley
1 garlic clove, minced
½ teaspoon oregano
½ teaspoon salt
½ teaspoon freshly ground pepper

1. Preheat the broiler. Broil the peppers 4 inches from the heat,
turning until the skin is blackened all over, about 10 minutes. Let
stand in a closed paper bag or covered in a bowl for 10 minutes.
Remove the stems and seeds and peel off the skins. Cut the peppers
into ½-inch strips.
2. Meanwhile, place the chicken in a large skillet. Add water to
cover and heat to a simmer. Reduce the heat to low and poach,
uncovered, until the chicken is white throughout, 7 to 9 minutes.
Remove the chicken, cover loosely and let stand until cool enough
to handle. Cut the chicken into ½-inch pieces.
3. Blanch the corn kernels in a medium saucepan of boiling water
until crisp-tender, about 2 minutes. Drain and cool under cold
running water; drain again.
4. In a large bowl, combine the roasted peppers, chicken, corn and
scallion. Toss to mix.
5. In a small bowl, whisk together the vinegar, olive oil, parsley,
garlic, oregano, salt and pepper. Pour over the chicken mixture and
toss gently to coat. Let stand at room temperature, loosely covered,
for 30 to 60 minutes to allow the flavors to blend before serving.

Calories: 271	Protein: 36 gm	Total Fat: 8 gm
Saturated Fat: 2 gm	Cholesterol: 88 mg	Carbohydrates: 15 gm
Sodium: 357 mg		

A SUPER SOURCE OF:

Phosphorus	━━━━━━ 26%	
Vitamin A	━━━━━━━ 34%	
Niacin	━━━━━━━━━━ 55%	
Vitamin C	━━━━━━━━━━━━━━━━━━ 100%	

0%   U.S. Recommended Daily Allowance   100%

CHICKEN AND PASTA

Chicken and pasta—two of America's favorite foods—make healthy bedfellows: a complete protein combined with a complex carbohydrate. Chicken is high in protein and is a source of Vitamin A, B vitamins, iron, phosphorus and calcium. Pasta is high in carbohydrates, fiber and a source of B vitamins. It's also low in calories, sodium, cholesterol and fat. It's probably one of the happier marriages around.

The sauces on pasta are what give it its villainous high-fat status. These recipes fix that problem by substituting olive oil in small amounts for butter and cream and by using tomatoes, chicken broth or the pasta cooking liquid to sauce the pasta.

Pasta is the perfect vehicle when combined with chicken in such dishes as the classic Chinese Chicken Sesame Noodles and Spaghetti Bolognese (made with ground chicken) instead of beef or pork, to the trendy Chicken and Shells with Sun-Dried Tomatoes.

Remember to cook the pasta in a large pot of water brought to boiling, then add salt and cook, stirring occasionally, until *al dente,* or tender but firm to the bite, usually 10 to 12 minutes for dried pasta. Drain, reserving some of the pasta liquid if called for, and toss immediately with the sauce and other ingredients.

*P*enne with Chicken, Tomatoes and Mozzarella

4 SERVINGS

¾ pound skinless, boneless chicken breast halves
1½ teaspoons olive oil
1 large onion, finely chopped (about 1 cup)
1 garlic clove, crushed
1 can (28 ounces) Italian peeled tomatoes, with their juice
¼ teaspoon crushed hot pepper flakes
10 ounces penne or other tubular pasta
3 ounces part-skim mozzarella cheese, finely diced
1 tablespoon chopped parsley
Grated Parmesan cheese (optional)

1. Place the chicken in a large skillet. Add water to cover and heat to a simmer. Reduce the heat to low and poach, uncovered, until the chicken is white throughout, 7 to 9 minutes. Remove the chicken, cover loosely and let stand until cool enough to handle. Cut the chicken into ½-inch dice.

2. In a large nonstick skillet, heat the olive oil over medium heat. Add the onion and garlic and cook, stirring occasionally, until softened, about 5 minutes. Add the tomatoes with their juice and the hot pepper and cook over medium-high heat until the sauce is thickened, 15 to 20 minutes.

3. Meanwhile, cook the penne in a large pot of boiling salted water according to package directions; drain. Toss with the sauce and chicken in a large bowl. Add the mozzarella cheese and parsley and toss again. Pass a bowl of grated Parmesan cheese, if desired.

Calories: 491   Protein: 37 gm   Total Fat: 9 gm
Saturated Fat: 3 gm   Cholesterol: 66 mg   Carbohydrates: 65 gm
Sodium: 472 mg

A SUPER SOURCE OF:

Calcium	22%
Phosphorus	37%
Iron	27%
Vitamin A	29%
Thiamin	57%
Riboflavin	29%
Niacin	64%
Vitamin C	57%

0%   U.S. Recommended Daily Allowance   100%

Chicken and Orzo Provençal

4 SERVINGS

¼ *cup pine nuts*
3 *cups no-salt chicken broth*
1 *cup orzo*
2 *teaspoons olive oil*
½ *cup finely chopped shallots*
½ *cup finely chopped green bell pepper*
1 *garlic clove, minced*
2 *cups diced cooked chicken (about ½ pound)*
2 *tablespoons sun-dried tomato bits*
2 *tablespoons pitted Niçoise olives*
2 *tablespoons balsamic or red wine vinegar*
1 *teaspoon capers, rinsed and drained*
¼ *cup grated Parmesan cheese*
⅓ *cup shredded fresh basil*
½ *teaspoon freshly ground pepper*

1. In a small skillet, toast the pine nuts over medium heat, shaking the pan frequently, until browned, 3 to 5 minutes; set aside.

2. In a large saucepan, bring the chicken broth to a boil. Add the orzo and cook until just tender, 10 to 12 minutes. Remove from the heat and let stand, covered.

3. Meanwhile, in a medium nonstick skillet, heat the olive oil over medium heat. Add the shallots, bell pepper and garlic. Cook, stirring occasionally, 2 to 3 minutes. Add the chicken, sun-dried tomatoes, olives, vinegar and capers. Cook, stirring occasionally, 3 minutes.

4. Add the chicken mixture to the orzo and stir to mix. Add the cheese, basil, pine nuts and pepper and toss to combine. Serve warm or at room temperature.

Calories: 453	Protein: 30 gm	Total Fat: 16 gm
Saturated Fat: 4 gm	Cholesterol: 54 mg	Carbohydrates: 48 gm
Sodium: 359 mg		

A SUPER SOURCE OF:

Phosphorus	━━━━━━━	31%
Iron	━━━━━━━	30%
Thiamin	━━━━━━━━━━	44%
Riboflavin	━━━━━	24%
Niacin	━━━━━━━━━━━━	54%
Vitamin C	━━━━━━━━━━	44%

0%   U.S. Recommended Daily Allowance   100%

Chinese Chicken Sesame Noodles

4 SERVINGS

½ *pound dried Chinese noodles or thin spaghetti*
1 *teaspoon Asian sesame oil*
1 *pound skinless, boneless chicken breast halves*
2 *tablespoons sesame seeds*
¼ *cup creamy peanut butter*
¼ *cup no-salt chicken broth*
1 *tablespoon reduced-sodium soy sauce or tamari*
1 *tablespoon rice wine vinegar*
1 *teaspoon grated fresh ginger*
1 *teaspoon Chinese chili paste with garlic*
2 *scallions, thinly sliced*
¼ *cup chopped fresh coriander or parsley*
1 *cucumber, peeled, seeded and cut into 3 × ¼-inch strips*
6 *ounces bean sprouts, rinsed and drained*

1. In a large pot of boiling salted water, cook the noodles according to package directions; drain and pat dry. Transfer to a large bowl and toss with the sesame oil; cover and let stand at room temperature.

2. Place the chicken in a large skillet. Add water to cover and heat to a simmer. Reduce the heat to low and poach, uncovered, until the chicken is white throughout, 7 to 9 minutes. Remove the chicken, cover loosely and let stand until cool enough to handle. Cut the chicken into thin strips.

3. Meanwhile, in a small skillet, toast the sesame seeds over medium heat, stirring frequently until browned, 3 to 5 minutes; set aside.

4. In a medium bowl, combine the peanut butter, chicken broth, soy sauce, vinegar, ginger and chili paste. Whisk until blended.

5. Add the chicken, scallions and coriander to the noodles. Pour the peanut dressing over all and toss until coated. Divide the noodles among 4 serving plates and top with the cucumber, bean sprouts and sesame seeds.

Calories: 497	Protein: 41 gm	Total Fat: 14 gm
Saturated Fat: 2 gm	Cholesterol: 66 mg	Carbohydrates: 52 gm
Sodium: 322 mg		

A SUPER SOURCE OF:

Phosphorus	▬▬▬▬▬▬ 44%
Iron	▬▬▬▬ 27%
Thiamin	▬▬▬▬▬▬ 49%
Riboflavin	▬▬▬▬ 26%
Niacin	▬▬▬▬▬▬▬▬▬▬▬▬ 100%
Vitamin C	▬▬▬▬ 28%

0%   U.S. Recommended Daily Allowance   100%

According to the Human Nutrition Information Service, 3½ ounces (100 grams) of cooked white meat chicken without skin contains 173 calories, 30.9 grams protein and 4.5 grams fat 3½ ounces (100 grams) of cooked white meat chicken with skin contains 222 calories, 29 grams protein and 10.9 grams fat 3½ ounces (100 grams) of cooked dark meat chicken without skin contains 205 calories, 27.4 grams protein and 9.7 grams fat 3½ ounces (100 grams) of cooked dark meat chicken with skin contains 253 calories, 26.0 grams protein, 15.8 grams fat.

Spaghetti Bolognese

4 SERVINGS

2 teaspoons olive oil
½ pound ground chicken
1 small onion, chopped
1 small green bell pepper, chopped
1 garlic clove, crushed
1 can (28 ounces) Italian peeled tomatoes, with their juice
1 tablespoon chopped fresh basil, or 1 teaspoon dried
½ teaspoon oregano
½ teaspoon salt
¼ teaspoon freshly ground pepper
12 ounces spaghetti
Grated Parmesan cheese (optional)

1. In a medium nonstick skillet, heat 1 teaspoon of the olive oil over medium heat. Add the chicken and cook, breaking up any lumps with the back of a spoon, until no longer pink, about 5 minutes. Remove with a slotted spoon; set aside.
2. In the same skillet, heat the remaining 1 teaspoon olive oil over medium heat. Add the onion, bell pepper and garlic. Cook until softened, about 5 minutes. Add the reserved chicken, tomatoes with their juice, basil, oregano, salt and pepper. Cook, breaking up the tomatoes with the back of a spoon, until thickened, about 30 minutes.
3. Meanwhile, cook the spaghetti in a large pot of boiling salted water according to package directions; drain. Divide the spaghetti among 4 serving bowls. Top with the spaghetti sauce. Sprinkle with Parmesan cheese, if desired.

Calories: 473   Protein: 23 gm   Total Fat: 9 gm
Saturated Fat: 2 gm   Cholesterol: 47 mg   Carbohydrates: 74 gm
Sodium: 650 mg

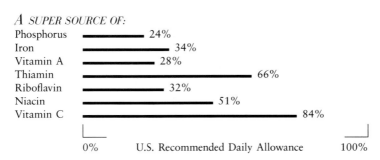

A SUPER SOURCE OF:

Phosphorus	24%
Iron	34%
Vitamin A	28%
Thiamin	66%
Riboflavin	32%
Niacin	51%
Vitamin C	84%

0%   U.S. Recommended Daily Allowance   100%

Chicken Lo Mein

4 SERVINGS

½ pound Chinese egg noodles or thin spaghetti
1 teaspoon Asian sesame oil
½ cup no-salt chicken broth
1 tablespoon oyster sauce
2 teaspoons reduced-sodium soy sauce
1 teaspoon rice wine vinegar
1 teaspoon cornstarch
½ teaspoon sugar
½ teaspoon crushed hot pepper flakes
1 tablespoon plus 1 teaspoon vegetable oil
1 red bell pepper, cut into ¼-inch strips
2 cups sliced bok choy or cabbage
2 scallions, sliced
1 teaspoon minced fresh ginger
2 garlic cloves, minced
2 cups shredded cooked chicken (about ½ pound)

1. Cook the noodles in a large pot of boiling salted water according to package directions. Drain and pat dry. Transfer to a medium bowl and toss with the sesame oil.
2. In a small bowl, whisk together the chicken broth, oyster sauce, soy sauce, vinegar, cornstarch, sugar and hot pepper flakes. Set the sauce aside.
3. In a large nonstick skillet or wok, heat 1 teaspoon of the vegetable oil over medium-high heat. Add the bell pepper and bok choy and cook, stirring constantly, until crisp-tender, about 3 minutes. With a slotted spoon, transfer to a bowl.
4. Heat the remaining 1 tablespoon oil in the skillet. Add the scallions, ginger and garlic and cook, stirring constantly, 1 minute. Add the noodles and cook, stirring constantly, 1 minute longer. Add the sauce and cook, stirring, 2 minutes. Add the vegetables and chicken and cook, stirring, until hot, 2 minutes longer.

Calories: 403	Protein: 26 gm	Total Fat: 13 gm
Saturated Fat: 2 gm	Cholesterol: 104 mg	Carbohydrates: 46 gm
Sodium: 370 mg		

A SUPER SOURCE OF:

Phosphorus	26%
Iron	24%
Vitamin A	53%
Thiamin	43%
Niacin	53%
Vitamin C	92%

0%   U.S. Recommended Daily Allowance   100%

*O*recchiette with Lemon Chicken Sauce

Orecchiette, or "little ears," are round, small disk-shaped pasta. If unavailable in your supermarket, substitute radiatore, a rippled pasta shape that looks like a radiator, or shell-shaped pasta.

4 SERVINGS

½ *pound orecchiette, radiatore or pasta shells*
1 *pound fresh plum tomatoes, seeded and diced (about 2 cups)*
2 *cups diced cooked chicken (about ½ pound)*
2 *ounces Niçoise olives, pitted and halved*
3 *tablespoons fresh lemon juice*
2 *tablespoons olive oil*
1 *teaspoon grated lemon zest*
¼ *teaspoon salt*
½ *teaspoon freshly ground pepper*
¼ *cup chopped parsley*
¼ *cup grated Parmesan cheese*

1. Cook the pasta in a large saucepan of boiling salted water, according to package directions. Scoop out and reserve ½ cup of the pasta cooking liquid. Drain the pasta.
2. Meanwhile, in a large bowl, combine the tomatoes, chicken and olives. Toss to mix.
3. In a small bowl, whisk together the lemon juice, olive oil, lemon zest, salt and pepper. Pour over the tomato mixture and toss to combine. Add the hot pasta and toss. Add as much of the reserved pasta liquid as needed to make a saucy consistency. Sprinkle with the parsley and cheese.

Calories: 466	Protein: 27 gm	Total Fat: 18 gm
Saturated Fat: 4 gm	Cholesterol: 54 mg	Carbohydrates: 50 gm
Sodium: 665 mg		

A SUPER SOURCE OF:

Phosphorus	27%
Iron	22%
Vitamin A	31%
Thiamin	45%
Riboflavin	24%
Niacin	51%
Vitamin C	49%

0%   U.S. Recommended Daily Allowance   100%

Chicken with Farfel

4 SERVINGS

½ pound farfel, barley shapes or orzo
1 cup chopped peeled carrot
1 tablespoon vegetable oil
1 large onion, chopped (about 1 cup)
½ cup chopped green bell pepper
½ pound fresh mushrooms, chopped (about 2 cups)
2 cups diced cooked chicken (about ½ pound)
¼ cup no-salt chicken broth
½ teaspoon salt
¼ teaspoon freshly ground pepper
¼ cup chopped parsley

1. Cook the farfel in a medium pot of boiling salted water according to package directions; drain.
2. Meanwhile, blanch the carrots in a small saucepan in boiling water until tender, 3 minutes; drain.
3. In a large nonstick skillet, heat the oil over medium heat. Add the onion and bell pepper and cook, stirring frequently, until softened, about 5 minutes. Add the carrot and cook, stirring frequently, 2 minutes.
4. Add the mushrooms and cook, stirring frequently, until the liquid they give off is absorbed, 3 to 5 minutes.
5. Add the farfel and chicken; stir to combine. Pour in the broth, increase the heat to medium-high and cook, stirring frequently, until all the liquid is absorbed and the mixture is lightly browned, 10 to 12 minutes. Sprinkle with the salt, pepper and parsley.

Calories: 395	Protein: 26 gm	Total Fat: 9 gm
Saturated Fat: 2 gm	Cholesterol: 50 mg	Carbohydrates: 52 gm
Sodium: 344 mg		

A SUPER SOURCE OF:

Phosphorus	■■■■■■	28%
Iron	■■■■■	24%
Vitamin A	■■■■■■■■■■■■■■■■■■■■■■■	100%
Thiamin	■■■■■■■■■■■	47%
Riboflavin	■■■■■■■■	35%
Niacin	■■■■■■■■■■■■■	61%
Vitamin C	■■■■■■■■■■■	45%

0%   U.S. Recommended Daily Allowance   100%

Chicken Pasta Primavera

Fresh seasonal vegetables, quickly cooked, and poached chicken make up this healthy version of pasta primavera. 6 SERVINGS

½ pound skinless, boneless chicken breast halves
2 ounces pine nuts
1 zucchini (about 6 ounces), cut into 2½ × ¼-inch strips
1 summer squash (about 6 ounces), cut into 2½ × ¼-inch strips
6 asparagus spears, trimmed (about 4 ounces), cut into 2-inch pieces
2 cups broccoli florets
⅓ cup fresh or frozen peas
2 tablespoons olive oil
½ cup chopped onion
2 garlic cloves, minced
1 pound fresh plum tomatoes, seeded and cut into ½-inch dice (about 2 cups)
½ teaspoon salt
¼ teaspoon freshly ground pepper
⅓ cup chopped fresh basil
1 pound spaghetti
¼ cup grated Parmesan cheese
½ teaspoon crushed hot pepper flakes

1. Place the chicken in a large skillet. Add water to cover and heat to a simmer. Reduce the heat to low and poach, uncovered, until the chicken is white throughout, 7 to 8 minutes. Remove the chicken, cover loosely and let stand until cool enough to handle. Shred the chicken into strips.

2. Meanwhile, in a small skillet, toast the pine nuts over medium heat, shaking the pan frequently, until browned, 3 to 5 minutes; set aside.

3. In a medium saucepan of boiling salted water, blanch each vegetable until just crisp-tender; 3 minutes for the zucchini and squash, 5 minutes for the asparagus and broccoli and 1 minute for the peas; drain well. In a large bowl, combine all the vegetables.

4. In a large nonstick skillet, heat 1 tablespoon of the olive oil over medium heat. Add the onion and garlic and cook, stirring frequently, until softened, 3 to 5 minutes. Add the tomatoes, salt and pepper. Cook, stirring frequently, 3 minutes. Add the vegetables to the sauce. Stir in the basil.

5. Cook the spaghetti in a large saucepan of boiling water according to package directions. Scoop out and reserve ½ cup of the cooking water. Drain the pasta.

6. Meanwhile, heat the reserved pasta cooking water, remaining 1 tablespoon olive oil and cheese in a small saucepan. Toss the hot pasta and cheese mixture with the vegetables. Sprinkle with the pine nuts and hot pepper flakes and toss again.

Calories: 486   Protein: 26 gm   Total Fat: 13 gm
Saturated Fat: 2 gm   Cholesterol: 26 mg   Carbohydrates: 69 gm
Sodium: 26 mg

A SUPER SOURCE OF:

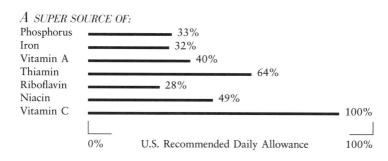

Phosphorus   33%
Iron   32%
Vitamin A   40%
Thiamin   64%
Riboflavin   28%
Niacin   49%
Vitamin C   100%

0%   U.S. Recommended Daily Allowance   100%

To reduce the consumption of saturated fat in your diet, choose foods relatively low in this and cholesterol, such as fruits, vegetables, whole grain breads, cereals, fish, poultry, lean meats and low-fat dairy products.

Chicken and Shells with Sun-Dried Tomatoes

Although the recipe calls for only 1 cup, this sauce works best when made in a 3-cup batch. Freeze the remaining 2 cups in 1-cup portions for future use. 6 SERVINGS

1 pound medium pasta shells
1 can (14 ounces) Italian peeled tomatoes, with their juice
1 jar (3 ounces) sun-dried tomato bits (about 1 cup)
½ cup no-salt chicken broth
¼ cup finely chopped shallots or onion
1 garlic clove, chopped
2 tablespoons chopped fresh basil or 1 teaspoon dried
1 tablespoon olive oil
1 tablespoon fresh lemon juice
1 teaspoon oregano
½ teaspoon salt
¼ teaspoon freshly ground pepper
3 cups diced (½-inch) cooked chicken (about ¾ pound)
1 yellow or red bell pepper, finely diced
¼ cup grated Parmesan cheese

1. Cook the shells in a large pot of boiling salted water according to package directions. Scoop out and reserve ½ cup of the pasta cooking liquid. Drain the shells.

2. In a food processor, process the tomatoes with their juice, sun-dried tomato bits, chicken broth, shallots, garlic, basil, olive oil, lemon juice, oregano, salt and pepper. Process until mixture is well blended.

3. In a large bowl, toss the hot pasta with the chicken, bell pepper, 1 cup of the sauce and the pasta cooking liquid until well mixed. Divide the pasta among 4 serving bowls; sprinkle each with 1 tablespoon Parmesan cheese.

Calories: 496   Protein: 31 gm   Total Fat: 9 gm
Saturated Fat: 2 gm   Cholesterol: 53 mg   Carbohydrates: 73 gm
Sodium: 431 mg

A SUPER SOURCE OF:

Phosphorus	▬▬▬▬▬ 33%
Iron	▬▬▬▬▬ 32%
Vitamin A	▬▬▬▬▬▬▬▬▬▬▬ 79%
Thiamin	▬▬▬▬▬▬▬▬▬ 65%
Riboflavin	▬▬▬▬▬ 34%
Niacin	▬▬▬▬▬▬▬▬▬ 65%
Vitamin C	▬▬▬▬▬▬▬▬▬▬▬▬▬ 100%

0%   U.S. Recommended Daily Allowance   100%

A 3½-ounce portion of skinless chicken contains 29 grams protein, about one half the daily adult requirement.

CHICKEN AND GRAINS

Grains come in many guises, as reflected by the international diversity of recipes in this chapter. They're an important staple in nearly every cuisine and a great complement to chicken. Following is a mini-glossary for those grains used in this chapter.

***Basmati (Indian)* or *Texmati (American)* Rice:** Light and fluffy with a slightly sticky texture—used in the Aromatic Afghan Rice with Chicken.

Arborio Rice: A short-grain Italian rice that forms a creamy texture by simmering and stirring to form Spring Vegetables and Chicken Risotto.

Long-Grain White Rice: Most commonly found in America, the grains of this rice remain separate when properly cooked, so it is fluffy and tender. It is the main component of the Creole dish Chicken and Shrimp Jambalaya.

Long-Grain Brown Rice: Cooks up fluffy with a distinctive grainy texture and nutty flavor. It is lower in calories than white rice. Used as leftovers in the Fried Brown Rice with Chicken.

Bulgur: Finely ground wheatberries that can be used by just pouring boiling water over it. Great for no-cook dishes, especially during the long hot days of summer.

Cornmeal: Made from corn that is dried and then ground. White and yellow cornmeal is interchangeable. Here it's cooked until it's creamy and soft and serves as a base for Polenta with Chicken-Shiitake Sauce.

Couscous: Semolina made from durum wheat that has been steamed and dried. It comes in fine, medium and coarse grinds. I used the quick-cooking variety, which is what is sold as couscous in the supermarket. Here it is tossed with fresh coriander and toasted almonds and served an accompaniment to the Moroccan Chicken.

*F*ried Brown Rice with Chicken

This is a great dish that can be made from leftovers. 4 SERVINGS

1 large egg
2 teaspoons Asian sesame oil
1 tablespoon vegetable oil
2 scallions, sliced
3 cups cooked brown rice
½ pound cooked chicken breasts, cut into strips
½ cup frozen peas, defrosted
1 ounce low-fat turkey ham, cut into strips
1 tablespoon reduced-sodium soy sauce
2 tablespoons chopped parsley
1 tablespoon sesame seeds

1. In a small bowl, beat the egg with 1 tablespoon water until blended.
2. In a small nonstick skillet, heat 1 teaspoon of the sesame oil over medium heat. Add the beaten egg and cook, stirring constantly, until scrambled to medium-firm, about 3 minutes. Transfer to a small plate. Break the egg into pieces and set aside.
3. In a large nonstick skillet, heat the vegetable oil over medium-high heat. Add the scallions and cook 1 minute. Add the brown rice and cook, stirring, just until heated through, 2 to 3 minutes. Add the chicken, peas, turkey ham and soy sauce. Cook until heated through, 2 to 3 minutes. Add the remaining 1 teaspoon sesame oil and toss. Garnish with the egg, parsley and sesame seeds.

Calories: 366	Protein: 26 gm	Total Fat: 12 gm
Saturated Fat: 2 gm	Cholesterol: 101 mg	Carbohydrates: 38 gm
Sodium: 307 mg		

A SUPER SOURCE OF:
Phosphorus ━━━━━━ 32%
Niacin ━━━━━━━━━━ 54%

0%   U.S. Recommended Daily Allowance   100%

*A*romatic Afghan Rice with Chicken

Caravan, an Afghan restaurant in the theater district in New York, was the inspiration for this flavorful complex dish. 4 SERVINGS

¼ *teaspoon saffron threads*
2 *cups no-salt chicken broth, hot*
1 *tablespoon vegetable oil*
½ *cup chopped onion*
1 *cinnamon stick*
2 *tablespoons sugar*
⅛ *teaspoon ground cloves*
⅛ *teaspoon ground cardamom*
1 *cup basmati, Texmati or long-grain white rice*
2 *tablespoons orange juice*
½ *teaspoon salt*
2 *tablespoons julienne strips orange zest*
2 *cups shredded cooked chicken (about ½ pound)*
1 *ounce slivered almonds*
1 *ounce shelled unsalted pistachio nuts*
2 *tablespoons currants or raisins*

1. In a small bowl, combine the saffron and 2 tablespoons of the broth. Let stand until ready to use.
2. In a large saucepan, heat the oil over medium heat. Add the onion and cook, stirring frequently, until golden, 7 to 10 minutes. Add the cinnamon stick, sugar, cloves and cardamom. Cook, stirring constantly, 1 minute, to toast the spices. Add the rice and cook, stirring, until opaque, 1 to 2 minutes. Add the remaining broth, the orange juice and the salt. Heat to boiling. Add the dissolved saffron and the orange zest. Reduce the heat to low, cover and cook until the liquid is absorbed, about 15 minutes.
3. Stir in the chicken and let stand, covered, 10 minutes. Just before serving, add the almonds, pistachios and currants and stir to mix.

Calories: 456	Protein: 24 gm	Total Fat: 16 gm
Saturated Fat: 3 gm	Cholesterol: 50 mg	Carbohydrates: 54 gm
Sodium: 354 mg		

A SUPER SOURCE OF:

Phosphorus	━━━━━ 25%	
Iron	━━━━ 23%	
Thiamin	━━━━━ 25%	
Niacin	━━━━━━━ 42%	

0%   U.S. Recommended Daily Allowance   100%

Spring Vegetables and Chicken Risotto

Depending on the rest of your menu, this elegant dish can be offered as a main dish or as a first course, in which case it will serve up to 8. 6 SERVINGS

½ teaspoon saffron threads
6 cups no-salt chicken broth, hot
½ pound fresh asparagus, trimmed and cut into ½-inch pieces
1 tablespoon olive oil
¼ teaspoon chopped shallots or onion
2 cups Arborio rice
4 cups diced cooked chicken (about 1 pound)
4 ounces yellow squash, cut into ½-inch dice
4 ounces zucchini, cut into ½-inch dice
2 tablespoons chopped fresh chives
½ cup shredded fresh basil
¼ cup grated Parmesan cheese
½ teaspoon salt
¼ teaspoon freshly ground pepper

1. In a small bowl, combine the saffron with 2 tablespoons of the chicken broth. Let stand until ready to use.
2. Blanch the asparagus in a small saucepan of boiling water until crisp-tender, 3 to 5 minutes; drain and set aside.
3. In a large saucepan, heat the oil over low heat. Add the shallots and cook until softened, 2 to 3 minutes. Add the rice and stir to coat. Increase the heat to medium, add ½ cup of the hot broth, and cook rice, stirring constantly, until the liquid is almost absorbed. Repeat, adding the remaining broth ½ cup at a time, until the rice is tender and the dish has a creamy consistency, about 25 minutes.
3. Stir in the saffron, chicken, asparagus, squash, zucchini and chives. Cook for 5 minutes. Remove from the heat. Add the basil, cheese, salt and pepper; stir to combine. Serve immediately.

Calories: 463	Protein: 31 gm	Total Fat: 11 gm
Saturated Fat: 3 gm	Cholesterol: 70 mg	Carbohydrates: 58 gm
Sodium: 365 mg		

A SUPER SOURCE OF:

Phosphorus	▬▬▬	27%
Iron	▬▬▬	31%
Thiamin	▬▬▬	32%
Niacin	▬▬▬▬▬	58%

0%   U.S. Recommended Daily Allowance   100%

Polenta with Chicken-Shiitake Sauce

4 SERVINGS

2 teaspoons olive oil
½ cup chopped onion
1 garlic clove, minced
½ pound shiitake mushrooms, stemmed, rinsed and sliced
½ pound ground chicken
1 can (14 ounces) Italian peeled tomatoes, coarsely
  chopped, with their juice
1 tablespoon chopped fresh basil or ½ teaspoon dried
½ teaspoon salt
½ teaspoon freshly ground pepper
2½ cups no-salt chicken broth
½ cup fine yellow cornmeal
2 tablespoons grated Parmesan cheese
2 tablespoons chopped parsley
1 tablespoon unsalted butter

1. In a large nonstick skillet, heat the olive oil over medium heat. Add the onion and garlic and cook, stirring constantly, until softened, 2 to 3 minutes. Add the mushrooms and cook, stirring frequently, until softened, about 3 minutes. Add the chicken and cook, breaking up any lumps with the back of a spoon, until no longer pink, about 5 minutes. Add the tomatoes with their juice, the basil, salt and pepper. Reduce the heat to low and simmer until the sauce is thickened, about 20 minutes.

2. Meanwhile, in a large saucepan, heat the chicken broth to boiling. Gradually whisk the cornmeal into the boiling broth. Reduce the heat to low and cook, stirring constantly, until the mixture thickens, about 5 minutes. Stir in the cheese, parsley and butter. Cover and let stand 10 minutes.

3. To serve, divide the polenta among 4 plates. Spoon the chicken shiitake sauce on top. Serve immediately.

Calories: 270	Protein: 16 gm	Total Fat: 13 gm
Saturated Fat: 4 gm	Cholesterol: 57 mg	Carbohydrates: 23 gm
Sodium: 566 mg		

A SUPER SOURCE OF:

Iron	━━━━━	22%
Riboflavin	━━━━━━	30%
Niacin	━━━━━━━	36%
Vitamin C	━━━━━━━	37%

0%   U.S. Recommended Daily Allowance   100%

Chicken and Shrimp Jambalaya

Jambalaya is a classic New Orleans dish of full-bodied flavors.
This version is low in fat, too. 6 SERVINGS

1 tablespoon vegetable oil
1 large onion, finely chopped (about 1 cup)
1 large green bell pepper, diced
1 garlic clove, minced
2 ounces low-fat turkey ham, diced (about ½ cup)
1 cup long-grain white rice
½ teaspoon dried thyme leaves
½ teaspoon salt
½ teaspoon freshly ground black pepper
½ teaspoon cayenne pepper
2 cups no-salt chicken broth
1 can (16 ounces) whole peeled tomatoes, drained and
  chopped, juices reserved
½ pound medium shrimp, shelled and deveined
2 cups diced cooked chicken (about ½ pound)
¼ cup chopped parsley

1. In a large noncorrosive saucepan, heat the oil over medium heat. Add the onion, bell pepper and garlic and cook, stirring occasionally, until softened, 5 to 7 minutes. Add the turkey ham and rice and cook, stirring, until the rice is opaque, about 3 minutes. Add the thyme, salt, black pepper and cayenne. Cook 1 minute. Add the chicken broth and tomatoes and their juice and bring to a boil. Cover and cook for 10 minutes.
2. Add the shrimp and cook until pink and firm, about 5 minutes. Add the chicken and cook just until heated through, about 2 minutes. Garnish with the parsley.

Calories: 291   Protein: 23 gm   Total Fat: 7 gm
Saturated Fat: 2 gm   Cholesterol: 81 mg   Carbohydrates: 32 gm
Sodium: 500 mg

A SUPER SOURCE OF:
Phosphorus   ▬▬▬ 22%
Iron   ▬▬▬ 23%
Niacin   ▬▬▬▬ 35%
Vitamin C   ▬▬▬▬▬▬ 62%

0%   U.S. Recommended Daily Allowance   100%

Moroccan Chicken with Coriander Couscous

4 SERVINGS

1 ounce slivered almonds (about ¼ cup)
1 pound skinless, boneless chicken thighs, cut into 1-inch
   pieces
2 teaspoons vegetable oil
1 large onion, chopped (about 1 cup)
1 garlic clove, minced
1 cup diced carrot
1 cup diced zucchini
½ teaspoon ground cinnamon
½ teaspoon ground cumin
½ teaspoon ground coriander
½ teaspoon cayenne pepper
2 cups no-salt chicken broth
½ cup canned chick-peas, rinsed and drained
½ cup golden and/or dark raisins
2 teaspoons fresh lemon juice
½ teaspoon salt
¼ teaspoon freshly ground pepper
1 cup couscous
¼ cup chopped fresh coriander or parsley

1. In a small skillet, toast the almonds over medium heat, shaking the pan frequently, until browned, about 5 minutes; set aside.
2. Coat a large nonstick skillet with vegetable cooking spray and heat over medium-high heat. Add the chicken and cook, turning, until browned all over, about 5 minutes. Remove from the skillet; set aside.

3. In the same skillet, heat the oil over medium heat. Add onion and garlic and cook until softened, about 3 minutes. Add the carrot and zucchini and cook, stirring, 3 minutes. Add the cinnamon, cumin, ground coriander and cayenne. Cook, stirring, 1 minute to toast the spices. Add the chicken broth and heat to boiling. Reduce the heat, add the reserved chicken and simmer, covered, 20 minutes.

4. Add the chick-peas and raisins and cook, covered, 10 minutes. Stir in the lemon juice, salt and pepper. Uncover and boil over medium-high heat until the sauce is thickened, about 5 minutes.

5. In a medium saucepan, heat 1½ cups water to boiling. Stir in the couscous and remove from the heat. Let stand 5 minutes. Stir in the almonds and coriander and fluff lightly with a fork before serving with the chicken.

Calories: 501	Protein: 34 gm	Total Fat: 13 gm
Saturated Fat: 2 gm	Cholesterol: 94 mg	Carbohydrates: 64 gm
Sodium: 458 mg		

A SUPER SOURCE OF:

Phosphorus	▬▬▬▬▬	39%
Iron	▬▬▬	21%
Vitamin A	▬▬▬▬▬▬▬▬▬▬▬	100%
Riboflavin	▬▬▬	21%
Niacin	▬▬▬▬▬▬	52%
Vitamin C	▬▬▬	25%

0%   U.S. Recommended Daily Allowance   100%

The recommended daily intake of dietary fiber is 25 to 35 grams. Some examples are: ⅓ cup bran cereal-8.6 grams; 1 slice whole wheat bread-1.7 grams; 1 pear-5 grams; ½ cup blackberries -3.3 grams; ½ cup cooked carrots-1.5 grams, and ⅓ cup prunes-3.8 grams.

GRILLED AND BROILED CHICKEN

Broiling and grilling are methods of cooking chicken with intense dry heat, either in the oven broiler or on a gas or charcoal grill, where the surface of the meat is seared quickly and the inside stays moist.

It's easy to burn or dry out chicken—especially without the protective coating of its skin and because broilers and grills vary greatly. Always check the chicken throughout the cooking process and baste with a little of its marinade up until 5 minutes before the meat is done.

Traditionally foods were basted with marinades that could be very oily. The marinades in this chapter are made with fruit juices, chicken broth, vinegars, mustards, fresh herbs and spices, for gutsy flavors that deliver a lot of punch.

If using the broiler in an electric oven, keep the door open slightly to keep the air flowing evenly and prevent the buildup of heat in the oven. Gas ovens have built-in ventilation, so it's not necessary to keep the door open when cooking in these broilers.

When cooking outdoors on a grill, you can adjust the temperature and the heat more easily than in a broiler, and it will impart an additional smoky flavor to the food.

Jamaican Jerk Chicken Wings

The culinary term *jerk* refers to meats or poultry coated in a marinade of Jamaican herbs, spices and chiles, then barbecued.

4 SERVINGS

⅓ cup pineapple preserves
¼ cup unsweetened pineapple juice
1 tablespoon distilled white vinegar
1 tablespoon dark brown sugar
2 scallions, minced
2 garlic cloves, minced
2 hot green chiles, seeded and minced
½ teaspoon ground allspice
½ teaspoon ground ginger
½ teaspoon dried thyme leaves
½ teaspoon salt
½ teaspoon freshly ground pepper
¼ teaspoon cayenne pepper
16 chicken wingettes (about 2½ pounds), or 8 chicken wings separated, wing tips discarded

1. In a medium bowl, combine all the ingredients except the chicken wings. Stir to blend. Add the wings and toss to coat completely. Refrigerate, covered, 1 hour.
2. Preheat the oven to 400 degrees. Place the wings in a flameproof baking pan in a single layer and bake, basting with the pan drippings every 10 minutes, until browned, 30 to 35 minutes.
3. Heat the broiler. Transfer the pan to the broiler and broil 4 inches from the heat until the wings are glazed, about 2 minutes.

Calories: 415	Protein: 29 gm	Total Fat: 21 gm
Saturated Fat: 6 gm	Cholesterol: 90 mg	Carbohydrates: 26 gm
Sodium: 367 mg		

A SUPER SOURCE OF:

Niacin ━━━━━━━━ 37%
Vitamin C ━━━━━━━━━ 46%

0%   U.S. Recommended Daily Allowance   100%

Lime-Grilled Chicken with Pepper-Corn Relish

This crunchy fresh corn relish, made without any fat, goes great with the lime-marinated grilled chicken. To enhance the southwestern flavor of the chicken, add some mesquite chips to the fire.

4 SERVINGS

¼ cup fresh lime juice
2 teaspoons vegetable oil
1 teaspoon grated lime zest
1 teaspoon ground cumin
1 teaspoon salt
¼ teaspoon freshly ground pepper
⅜ teaspoon cayenne pepper
4 skinless, boneless chicken breast halves (4 ounces each)
½ cup cooked fresh or canned or frozen corn kernels
½ cup diced red bell pepper
½ cup diced carrot
½ cup diced jicama or radish
3 tablespoons thinly sliced scallions
1 tablespoon chopped fresh coriander or parsley

1. In a large bowl, whisk together 2 tablespoons of the lime juice, the oil, lime zest, cumin, ½ teaspoon of the salt, the pepper and ¼ teaspoon of the cayenne. Add the chicken and turn to coat. Refrigerate, covered, 30 minutes to 1 hour.

2. To make the relish, in a medium bowl, combine, the corn, bell pepper, carrot, jicama, scallions and remaining lime juice, salt and remaining ⅛ teaspoon cayenne. Stir to blend.

3. Light a hot fire or preheat the broiler. Remove the chicken from the marinade and grill or broil 4 inches from the heat, turning once, until browned outside and white throughout, 5 to 7 minutes. Serve hot, warm or at room temperature with the pepper-corn relish.

Calories: 184   Protein: 27 gm   Total Fat: 4 gm
Saturated Fat: 1 gm   Cholesterol: 70 mg   Carbohydrates: 9 gm
Sodium: 483 mg

A SUPER SOURCE OF:

Phosphorus	22%
Vitamin A	99%
Niacin	60%
Vitamin C	59%

0%   U.S. Recommended Daily Allowance   100%

Chicken Vegetable Kebabs

4 SERVINGS

1 large red onion, cut into 1-inch pieces
4 ounces zucchini, halved and cut into 1/2-inch slices
1 large red or yellow bell pepper, seeded and cut into
    1-inch pieces
1/2 pound skinless, boneless chicken breasts, cut into 1-inch
    pieces
4 ounces yellow summer squash, halved and cut into 1/2-
    inch slices
1 large green bell pepper, seeded and cut into 1-inch pieces
2 tablespoons fresh lemon juice
1 tablespoon no-salt chicken broth
2 teaspoons olive oil
2 teaspoons Dijon mustard
1/2 teaspoon ground cumin
1/2 teaspoon salt
1/4 teaspoon freshly ground black pepper
1/8 teaspoon cayenne pepper

1. Thread 4 skewers with the red onion, zucchini, yellow bell
pepper, chicken, summer squash and green bell pepper, alternating
the ingredients. Place in a baking pan in a single layer.
2. In a small bowl, whisk together the lemon juice, chicken broth,
olive oil, mustard, cumin, salt, black pepper and cayenne. Pour over
the skewers and turn them to coat. Refrigerate, covered, 30 minutes
to 1 hour.
3. Light a hot fire in a grill or preheat the broiler. Grill or broil the
kebabs 4 inches from the heat, turning until they are browned all
over and the chicken is cooked through, about 10 minutes.

Calories: 118   Protein: 14 gm   Total Fat: 3 gm
Saturated Fat: 1 gm   Cholesterol: 36 mg   Carbohydrates: 8 gm
Sodium: 208 mg

A SUPER SOURCE OF:
Vitamin A   ━━━━━━━━━ 35%
Niacin   ━━━━━━━━ 31%
Vitamin C   ━━━━━━━━━━━━━━━━━━━━━━━━━━━ 100%
           └─   ─┘
           0%   U.S. Recommended Daily Allowance   100%

Oriental Glazed Chicken

Hoisin sauce is a sweet bean paste with a salty-sweet flavor used as a dipping sauce with Peking duck, or as a marinade with meat and poultry. It is available in the Asian foods section of most supermarkets. 4 SERVINGS

¼ *cup hoisin sauce*
1 *tablespoon rice wine or dry sherry*
1 *tablespoon reduced-sodium soy sauce*
1 *tablespoon dark brown sugar*
1 *tablespoon fresh lemon juice*
1 *tablespoon grated fresh ginger*
2 *teaspoons Asian sesame oil*
1 *scallion, thinly sliced*
2 *garlic cloves, crushed*
4 *skinless, boneless chicken thighs (about 1½ pounds)*
1 *tablespoon sesame seeds*

1. In a large shallow bowl, combine the hoisin sauce, rice wine, soy sauce, brown sugar, lemon juice, ginger, sesame oil, scallion and garlic. Stir until well blended. Add the chicken thighs and turn to coat. Refrigerate, covered, 30 minutes to 1 hour.
2. Light a hot fire in a grill or preheat the broiler. Grill or broil the chicken 4 inches from the heat, turning once, until browned, 5 to 7 minutes per side. Sprinkle the sesame seeds over the chicken.

Calories: 314	Protein: 34 gm	Total Fat: 16 gm
Saturated Fat: 4 gm	Cholesterol: 122 mg	Carbohydrates: 6 gm
Sodium: 454 mg		

A SUPER SOURCE OF:
Phosphorus ━━━━━━ 26%
Niacin ━━━━━━━━━ 43%

0%   U.S. Recommended Daily Allowance   100%

Chicken Teriyaki

4 SERVINGS

2 tablespoons honey
1 tablespoon reduced-sodium soy sauce
1 tablespoon no-salt chicken broth
1 tablespoon rice wine or dry sherry
1 tablespoon minced fresh ginger
1 tablespoon minced scallion
1 garlic clove, crushed
1 teaspoon vegetable oil
4 skinless, boneless chicken breast halves (4 ounces each)

1. In a large shallow bowl, combine the honey, soy sauce, chicken broth, rice wine, ginger, scallion, garlic and oil. Stir until blended. Add the chicken and turn to coat. Refrigerate, covered, 30 minutes to 1 hour.
2. Light a hot fire in a grill or preheat the broiler. Remove the chicken from the marinade and grill or broil 4 inches from the heat, turning once, until browned, 5 to 7 minutes.

Calories: 176   Protein: 29 gm   Total Fat: 4 gm
Saturated Fat: 1 gm   Cholesterol: 78 mg   Carbohydrates: 5 gm
Sodium: 144 mg

A SUPER SOURCE OF:
Phosphorus   ━━━━━ 21%
Niacin   ━━━━━━━━━━━━━ 63%
|
0%   U.S. Recommended Daily Allowance   100%

Total dietary fat intake should be about 30 percent of total calories, and cholesterol should be limited to 250 to 300 milligrams a day.

Hawaiian Chicken
with Papaya-Pineapple Sauce

4 SERVINGS

½ cup plus 2 tablespoons unsweetened pineapple juice
1 tablespoon reduced-sodium soy sauce
1 tablespoon no-salt chicken broth
2 teaspoons vegetable oil
2 teaspoons Dijon mustard
1 scallion, minced
2 jalapeño peppers, seeded and minced, or ½ teaspoon
   cayenne pepper
1 garlic clove, crushed
1 teaspoon ground ginger
4 skinless, boneless chicken breast halves (4 ounces each)
1 papaya or mango, peeled, seeded and diced
1 teaspoon fresh lime juice
Lime wedges, for garnish

1. In a large shallow bowl, combine 2 tablespoons of the pineapple juice, the soy sauce, chicken broth, oil, mustard, scallion, half the jalapeños, the garlic and ½ teaspoon of the ginger. Stir to blend. Add the chicken and turn to coat. Refrigerate, covered, 30 minutes to 1 hour.

2. To make the sauce, place the papaya, remaining ½ cup pineapple juice, lime juice, remaining jalapeño pepper and ginger in a food processor and puree until smooth.

3. Light a hot fire in a grill or preheat the broiler. Remove the chicken from the marinade and grill or broil 4 inches from the heat, turning once, until browned, 5 to 7 minutes.

4. Meanwhile, in a small saucepan, heat the papaya sauce over low heat just until warm.

5. To serve, spoon the sauce onto 4 serving plates. Place the chicken on top of the sauce. Garnish with lime wedges.

Calories: 218	Protein: 29 gm	Total Fat: 5 gm
Saturated Fat: 1 gm	Cholesterol: 78 mg	Carbohydrates: 14 gm
Sodium: 184 mg		

A SUPER SOURCE OF:

Phosphorus	▬▬▬ 22%	
Vitamin A	▬▬▬▬▬ 34%	
Niacin	▬▬▬▬▬▬▬▬▬ 65%	
Vitamin C	▬▬▬▬▬▬▬▬▬▬▬▬▬▬ 100%	

0%   U.S. Recommended Daily Allowance   100%

*B*alsamic Grilled Chicken
with Pickling Spices

The honey in the marinade mellows and rounds out the sharp, spicy flavor of the vinegar and pickling spices. 4 SERVINGS

2 tablespoons balsamic vinegar
2 tablespoons honey
1 tablespoon olive oil
1 tablespoon no-salt chicken broth
2 teaspoons pickling spices
1 teaspoon dried thyme leaves
1 scallion, thinly sliced
2 garlic cloves, crushed
½ teaspoon salt
¼ teaspoon freshly ground pepper
4 skinless, boneless chicken breast halves (4 ounces each)

1. In a large shallow bowl, combine all the ingredients except the chicken. Stir to blend. Add the chicken and turn to coat. Refrigerate, covered, 30 minutes to 1 hour.
2. Light a fire in a grill or preheat the broiler. Remove the chicken from the marinade and grill or broil 4 inches from the heat, turning once, until browned outside and cooked through, 5 to 7 minutes. Serve hot, warm or at room temperature.

Calories: 171   Protein: 26 gm   Total Fat: 5 gm
Saturated Fat: 1 gm   Cholesterol: 70 mg   Carbohydrates: 5 gm
Sodium: 197 mg

A SUPER SOURCE OF:
Niacin   ━━━━━━━━━━━━━ 57%
⌞_____   _____⌟
0%   U.S. Recommended Daily Allowance   100%

According to the USDA, 4 ounces of cooked ground white meat chicken without skin is only 90 calories and has only 2 grams of fat. 4 ounces of cooked ground dark meat chicken without skin is only 97 calories and has 3½ grams of fat.

Peppery Grilled Chicken with Hot Vinegar Dip

Heating the vinegar brings all the flavors into focus. 4 SERVINGS

4 skinless, boneless chicken breast halves (4 ounces each)
1 teaspoon salt
½ teaspoon freshly ground black pepper
¼ teaspoon cayenne pepper
¼ teaspoon white wine vinegar
2 tablespoons honey
2 teaspoons olive oil
2 teaspoons minced garlic
½ teaspoon ground cumin
1 jalapeño pepper, seeded and finely minced

1. Season the chicken with ½ teaspoon of the salt, ¼ teaspoon of the black pepper and ⅛ teaspoon of the cayenne.
2. Light a hot fire in a grill or preheat the broiler. Grill or broil the chicken 4 inches from the heat, turning once, until browned outside and cooked through, 5 to 7 minutes.
3. Meanwhile, in a small saucepan, combine the vinegar, ¼ cup water, the honey, olive oil, garlic, cumin, jalapeño pepper and remaining ½ teaspoon salt, ¼ teaspoon black pepper and remaining ⅛ teaspoon cayenne. Warm over low heat, stirring until blended and hot, about 2 minutes. Serve the dip with the chicken.

Calories: 233	Protein: 27 gm	Total Fat: 9 gm
Saturated Fat: 2 gm	Cholesterol: 82 mg	Carbohydrates: 10 gm
Sodium: 631 mg		

A SUPER SOURCE OF:
Niacin ━━━━━━━━━━ 43%

└─   ─┘
0%   U.S. Recommended Daily Allowance   100%

Always broil meats or poultry on a rack or broiling pan so that any fat can drip off.

BRAISED AND BAKED

CHICKEN

Since both of these techniques require slower cooking—either in the oven or over a burner over low heat—I've combined them into one chapter.

With braising, the chicken pieces are browned first, usually in oil. To keep down fat and calories, these recipes use a nonstick skillet coated with vegetable cooking spray. Then aromatic vegetables, such as onion and garlic, and spices are sautéed in a little oil. The remaining ingredients are added and simmered until the chicken is tender, as with the Chicken Fricassee with Meatballs or the Chicken Sausage Gumbo.

Baking chicken in the form of a pie lends itself to combining a variety of ingredients and encasing them in a crust that can be as diverse as the ingredients themselves. Tex-Mex Tamale Pie uses cornmeal; B'stilla, the classic Moroccan pie, uses phyllo dough, which is naturally low in calories and becomes crisp and flaky as it bakes.

Chicken Fricassee with Meatballs

This dish was handed down to my mother from my grandmother, and then to me. My mother made it her own and it became a standard in our house. My version is made with skinless chicken thighs and the meatballs are made with ground chicken. Serve with egg noodles. 6 SERVINGS

¼ cup all-purpose flour
½ teaspoon salt
½ teaspoon freshly ground pepper
6 chicken thighs, skinned (about 1¼ pounds)
1 tablespoon vegetable oil
2 medium onions, chopped (about 1½ cups)
2 garlic cloves, crushed
1 tablespoon sweet paprika, preferably imported
1 cup canned crushed tomatoes
1 cup no-salt chicken broth
Meatballs (recipe follows)

On a large flat plate, combine the flour, salt and pepper. Dust the chicken in the seasoned flour; shake off any excess.

2. Coat a large nonstick skillet coated with vegetable cooking spray and heat over medium heat. Add the chicken and cook, turning, until browned, 5 minutes. Remove from the skillet and set aside.

3. Add oil to the same skillet and heat over medium heat. Add the onions and garlic and cook, stirring frequently, until golden brown, 8 to 10 minutes. Stir in the paprika and cook 1 to 2 minutes. Return the chicken to the pan. Add the tomatoes and chicken broth, reduce the heat and simmer, covered, 15 to 20 minutes.

4. Gently add the meatballs to the saucepan and simmer, loosely covered, for 30 minutes.

*M*eatballs

MAKES 24 MEATBALLS

¾ pound ground chicken
2 tablespoons grated onion
2 tablespoons plain dry bread crumbs
2 tablespoons chopped parsley
1 medium egg
½ teaspoon salt
¼ teaspoon freshly ground pepper

In a large bowl, combine all the ingredients. Mix until well blended. Using your hands, shape into 1-inch balls.

Calories: 244   Protein: 24 gm   Total Fat: 11 gm
Saturated Fat: 2 gm   Cholesterol: 123 mg   Carbohydrates: 12 gm
Sodium: 558 mg

A SUPER SOURCE OF:
Phosphorus   ━━━━━ 20%
Vitamin A   ━━━━━ 23%
Niacin   ━━━━━━ 34%
Vitamin C   ━━━━━ 25%

0%   U.S. Recommended Daily Allowance   100%

*T*amale Pie

6 SERVINGS

3 cups no-salt chicken broth
1 cup yellow cornmeal
2 tablespoons chopped parsley
2 teaspoons vegetable oil
½ cup chopped scallions
1 garlic clove, minced
1 medium green bell pepper, chopped
1 fresh or pickled jalapeño pepper, seeded and minced
2 teaspoons chili powder
1 pound ground chicken
1 can (16 ounces) whole peeled tomatoes, chopped, juices reserved
½ teaspoon salt
½ teaspoon freshly ground black pepper
½ teaspoon cayenne pepper
1 cup corn kernels
½ cup grated reduced-fat Cheddar or Monterey Jack cheese

1. Preheat the oven to 350 degrees. In a large saucepan, heat the chicken broth to boiling over medium heat. Gradually whisk in the cornmeal. Reduce the heat to low and cook, stirring constantly, until thick, about 10 minutes. Stir in the parsley.
2. In a large nonstick skillet, heat the oil over medium heat. Add the scallions, garlic, bell pepper and jalapeño pepper. Cook, stirring frequently, until softened, about 3 minutes. Add the chili powder and cook, stirring, 1 minute. Add the chicken and cook, breaking up any lumps with a spoon, until no longer pink, about 5 minutes. Add the tomatoes with their juice, the salt, black pepper and cayenne. Simmer 10 minutes. Stir in the corn.
4. Spread half the cornmeal on the bottom of a 1½-quart baking dish. Spoon the chicken mixture over the cornmeal. Spread the remaining cornmeal over the chicken to cover. Sprinkle the cheese over the top. Bake 30 minutes, or until golden brown.

Calories: 307	Protein: 21 gm	Total Fat: 12 gm
Saturated Fat: 3 gm	Cholesterol: 69 mg	Carbohydrates: 29 gm
Sodium: 475 mg		

A SUPER SOURCE OF:

Iron	▬▬▬ 22%	
Vitamin A	▬▬▬▬ 35%	
Niacin	▬▬▬▬ 31%	
Vitamin C	▬▬▬▬▬▬▬ 71%	

0%   U.S. Recommended Daily Allowance   100%

*T*andoori Chicken Thighs

4 SERVINGS

½ teaspoon saffron threads
¼ cup all-purpose flour
½ teaspoon salt
¼ teaspoon freshly ground black pepper
¾ teaspoon cayenne pepper
4 skinless, boneless chicken thighs (1¼ pounds)
2 teaspoons vegetable oil
1 large onion, chopped (about 1 cup)
2 garlic cloves, crushed
2 teaspoons grated fresh ginger
1 teaspoon curry powder
½ teaspoon ground ginger
½ teaspoon ground cumin
½ cup no-salt chicken broth
½ cup nonfat plain yogurt
¼ cup chopped fresh coriander or parsley
1 tablespoon fresh lemon juice

1. In a small bowl, combine the saffron and 2 tablespoons hot water. Let stand until ready to use.
2. On a large flat plate, combine the flour, salt, black pepper and ¼ teaspoon of the cayenne. Dust the chicken thighs with the seasoned flour; shake off any excess.
3. Coat a large nonstick skillet with vegetable cooking spray and heat over medium heat. Add the chicken and cook, turning, until browned, 5 to 7 minutes. Remove from the skillet and set aside.
4. In the same skillet, heat the oil over medium heat. Add the onion, garlic and ginger and cook until softened, about 5 minutes. Add the curry powder, ground ginger, cumin and remaining ½ teaspoon cayenne. Cook, stirring, 1 minute. Return the chicken to the skillet. Add the chicken broth and saffron mixture and heat to boiling. Reduce the heat and simmer until the chicken is cooked through, 12 to 15 minutes.
5. In a small bowl, combine the yogurt, coriander and lemon juice. Stir until blended. Spoon about ⅓ cup of the curry sauce into the yogurt mixture, then stir back into the skillet. Heat but do not allow to boil. Remove from the heat. Serve with basmati rice.

Calories: 262   Protein: 31 gm   Total Fat: 9 gm
Saturated Fat: 2 gm   Cholesterol: 118 mg   Carbohydrates: 13 gm
Sodium: 426 mg

A SUPER SOURCE OF:
Niacin ━━━━━━━━━━━━━━━ 49%

└─   ─┘
0%   U.S. Recommended Daily Allowance   100%

Chicken Tagine with Almonds and Prunes

Tagines are slow-simmered aromatic Moroccan meat or poultry stews, named for their cooking pot. This one is made with boneless, skinless chicken thighs, and the amount of oil traditionally used is greatly reduced. 4 SERVINGS

½ teaspoon saffron threads
4 skinless, boneless chicken thighs (1¼ pounds), cut into
1½-inch pieces
2 teaspoons olive oil
1 large onion, chopped (about 1 cup)
1 garlic clove, minced
1 teaspoon ground cinnamon
½ teaspoon ground ginger
2 cups no-salt chicken broth
½ teaspoon salt
½ teaspoon freshly ground pepper
6 ounces pitted prunes
1 cinnamon stick
Orange peel from 1 orange
1 teaspoon sugar
2 ounces whole blanched almonds (about ½ cup)
2 tablespoons chopped fresh mint or 1 teaspoon dried

1. In a small bowl, combine the saffron with 2 tablespoons hot water. Let stand until ready to use.
2. Coat a large nonstick skillet with vegetable cooking spray and heat over medium heat. Add the chicken and cook, turning, until browned all over, about 5 minutes. Remove from the skillet and set aside.
3. In the same skillet, heat the oil over medium heat. Add the onion and garlic and cook, stirring frequently, until softened, about 5 minutes. Add the ground cinnamon and ginger and cook, stirring, 1 minute. Add the chicken broth, saffron mixture, salt and pepper and heat to boiling. Reduce the heat, add the reserved chicken and simmer, covered, until the chicken is cooked through and tender, 25 to 30 minutes.
4. Meanwhile, put the prunes, cinnamon stick and orange peel in a small saucepan with enough water to cover. Bring to a boil over medium heat. Reduce the heat and simmer until the prunes are soft, 12 to 15 minutes.

5. With a slotted spoon, transfer the chicken and the prunes to a serving dish. Add the prune cooking liquid and sugar to the skillet with the sauce. Increase the heat to medium-high and boil until the sauce is reduced by half. Pour over the chicken and prunes. Sprinkle the almonds and mint on top.

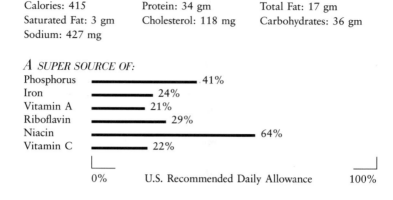

Calories: 415   Protein: 34 gm   Total Fat: 17 gm
Saturated Fat: 3 gm   Cholesterol: 118 mg   Carbohydrates: 36 gm
Sodium: 427 mg

A SUPER SOURCE OF:

Phosphorus	41%
Iron	24%
Vitamin A	21%
Riboflavin	29%
Niacin	64%
Vitamin C	22%

0%   U.S. Recommended Daily Allowance   100%

Chicken is a source of Vitamin A, B vitamins and minerals such as iron, zinc and phosphorus.

B'stilla

B'stilla, or *bisteeya*, is a savory, flaky, Moroccan pie, traditionally made with pigeon, eggs, almonds and spices. This version is made with poached shredded chicken, and vegetable cooking spray is substituted for melted butter between the layers of pastry.

4 TO 6 SERVINGS

½ teaspoon saffron threads
2 ounces whole blanched almonds
1 teaspoon granulated sugar
1¼ teaspoons ground cinnamon
1 tablespoon vegetable oil
2 medium onions, chopped (about 1½ cups)
1 teaspoon ground ginger
1 teaspoon ground turmeric
1½ cups no-salt chicken broth
¼ cup chopped parsley
2 large eggs, beaten
6 sheets of phyllo dough
2 cups shredded cooked chicken (about ½ pound)
1 teaspoon confectioners' sugar

1. Preheat the oven to 375 degrees. Lightly coat a 9 × 1½-inch round baking pan with vegetable cooking spray.

2. In a small bowl, combine the saffron with 2 tablespoons hot water. Let stand until ready to use.

3. In a small skillet, toast the almonds over medium heat, shaking pan frequently, until browned, about 5 minutes; set aside.

4. In a food processor, combine the almonds, granulated sugar and ¼ teaspoon of the cinnamon. Process until the almonds are finely ground.

5. In a large nonstick skillet, heat the oil over medium heat. Add the onions and cook, stirring frequently, until softened, about 5 minutes. Add the ginger and turmeric and cook, stirring, 1 minute. Add the chicken broth, saffron mixture and parsley. Heat to boiling and boil, stirring occasionally, 10 minutes. Add the eggs and cook, stirring, until set, 3 to 4 minutes. Remove from the heat; let drain in a sieve.

5. Arrange 1 sheet of phyllo dough to cover the bottom and sides of the prepared baking pan, allowing the sheet to extend over the sides. Spray the phyllo lightly with vegetable cooking spray. Repeat with 3 more sheets. Spread the almond mixture evenly over the phyllo dough. Spoon the egg mixture over the almond layer. Scatter the chicken over the eggs. Fold the ends of the phyllo dough, one at a time, over the filling, spraying each layer lightly with vegetable cooking spray. Place the remaining 2 sheets of phyllo dough over the center of the filling and tuck the ends under the bottom phyllo layer. Spray the top lightly with vegetable cooking spray.

6. **B**ake until the b'stilla is golden brown, 25 to 30 minutes. Invert onto a serving plate to unmold. Sprinkle the confectioners' sugar and remaining 1 teaspoon cinnamon over the top. Serve immediately.

Calories: 318	Protein: 22 gm	Total Fat: 15 gm
Saturated Fat: 3 gm	Cholesterol: 125 mg	Carbohydrates: 25 gm
Sodium: 185 mg		

A SUPER SOURCE OF:

Phosphorus ━━━━━ 20%
Riboflavin ━━━━━ 21%
Niacin ━━━━━━ 30%

0%   U.S. Recommended Daily Allowance   100%

Invest in a scale so you can serve sensible portions. The USDA recommends 4 ounces of poultry as a portion.

Chicken Sausage Gumbo

A stick-to-the-ribs stew, Louisiana style, made with chicken instead of pork sausage and spiced with cayenne pepper and hot pepper sauce. It's thickened with filé powder, ground dried sassafras leaves, available in the spice sections of the supermarket.

6 SERVINGS

1¼ pounds skinless, boneless chicken thighs, cut into 1½-inch pieces
½ pound chicken sausage
1 tablespoon vegetable oil
1 large onion, chopped (about 1 cup)
1 large green bell pepper, chopped (about 1 cup)
½ cup chopped celery
2 garlic cloves, minced
½ pound okra, trimmed and cut into ¼-inch slices (about 2 cups)
1 tablespoon all-purpose flour
½ teaspoon dried thyme leaves
½ teaspoon ground allspice
¼ teaspoon cayenne pepper
3 cups no-salt chicken broth
1 can (16 ounces) whole peeled tomatoes, drained and chopped
2 teaspoons Worcestershire sauce
1 bay leaf
1 teaspoon hot pepper sauce
½ teaspoon salt
½ teaspoon freshly ground pepper
¼ cup chopped parsley
1 teaspoon filé powder
6 cups cooked long-grain white rice

1. Coat a large nonstick skillet with vegetable cooking spray and heat over medium heat. Add the chicken and cook, turning, until browned all over, about 5 minutes. Remove from the skillet and set aside.
2. In the same skillet, heat ½ inch water to boiling. Add the sausage, reduce the heat to low and cook, covered, 10 minutes. Pour off the liquid; increase the heat to medium and cook the sausage, turning occasionally, until browned all over and no longer pink inside, 5 to 7 minutes. Cut the sausage into ½-inch slices.

3. In the same skillet, heat the oil over medium heat. Add the onion, bell pepper, celery and garlic. Cook, stirring frequently, until softened, about 5 minutes. Add the okra and cook, stirring frequently, until crisp-tender, about 3 minutes. Add the flour, thyme, allspice and cayenne and cook, stirring constantly, until browned, about 5 minutes. Carefully pour in the chicken broth and heat to boiling, whisking until thickened and smooth. Add the tomatoes, Worcestershire sauce and bay leaf. Cook, partially covered, until the gumbo is thickened, about 45 minutes. Add the chicken, chicken sausage, hot sauce, salt and pepper. Cook just until heated through. Remove from the heat and stir in the parsley and filé powder.

4. To serve, spoon the rice into 6 serving bowls. Ladle the gumbo over the rice.

Calories: 515	Protein: 34 gm	Total Fat: 10 gm
Saturated Fat: 2 gm	Cholesterol: 101 mg	Carbohydrates: 69 gm
Sodium: 663 mg		

A SUPER SOURCE OF:

Phosphorus	35%
Iron	32%
Vitamin A	21%
Thiamin	35%
Niacin	60%
Vitamin C	80%

0%   U.S. Recommended Daily Allowance   100%

Chicken Baked with Lemon and Basil

Marie Simmons, a great cook, my good friend and mentor from our days at *Cuisine* magazine, developed this simple but delectably delicious chicken dish. She suggests using fresh tarragon if fresh basil is unavailable. 4 SERVINGS

1 garlic clove, halved
4 bone-in chicken breast halves (2½ to 3 pounds in total),
trimmed of any excess fat and skin
4 large fresh basil leaves
½ teaspoon salt
¼ teaspoon freshly ground pepper
1 tablespoon olive oil
1 lemon, halved

1. Preheat the oven to 400 degrees. Rub the surface of a shallow baking dish with the cut side of the garlic; leave the garlic halves in the dish.
2. Place the chicken in prepared baking dish. Tuck a basil leaf under the skin of each piece of chicken; add the leafless basil stems to the dish. Season the chicken with the salt and pepper. Drizzle the olive oil over the chicken.
3. Squeeze the juice of 1 lemon half over the chicken. Cut the other half into 3 or 4 slices and arrange on top of the chicken.
4. Bake the chicken, turning once or twice and basting with pan juices, until browned and tender, about 35 minutes. Serve warm or at room temperature.

Calories: 261   Protein: 47 gm   Total Fat: 6 gm
Saturated Fat: 1 gm   Cholesterol: 118 mg   Carbohydrates: 3 gm
Sodium: 406 mg

A SUPER SOURCE OF:
Phosphorus   ━━━━━━━━━━━ 40%
Niacin   ━━━━━━━━━━━━━━━━━━━━━━━━━━━━ 100%
Vitamin C   ━━━━━━━━━ 39%

0%   U.S. Recommended Daily Allowance   100%

Cook chicken until meat is opaque and juices run clear, not pink. Pierce the thickest part with a fork or tip of a knife to see if juices run clear.

CORNISH GAME HENS

A Cornish game hen, chicken's closest cousin, is a cross between the hardy, fast-growing American white Plymouth Rock chicken and the flavorful English Cornish game hen. A game hen is small—between 1 and 2 pounds—and very tender.

According to Perdue Farms, Incorporated, 3½ ounces (100 grams) of cooked white meat Cornish hens with skin contains 202 calories, 24.6 grams protein and 11.5 grams fat; 3½ ounces (100 grams) of cooked dark meat Cornish hens with skin contains 246 calories, 24.4 grams protein and 16.4 grams fat.

Cornish hens cook quickly when split, especially when broiled or grilled, and each half is just the right size for an individual serving. They lend themselves to a variety of marinades, whether an apricot-orange glaze, ginger in triplicate, or soy sauce and Chinese five-spice powder.

*A*pricot-Orange Glazed Cornish Hens

4 SERVINGS

¼ cup apricot jam
¼ cup orange juice
2 tablespoons orange liqueur
1 tablespoon finely diced dried apricots
2 teaspoons finely diced orange zest
2 teaspoons white wine vinegar
½ teaspoon ground cinnamon
¼ teaspoon ground allspice
2 Cornish game hens (about 1¼ pounds each), backbone removed and halved

1. In a small bowl, combine all the ingredients except the hens. Stir the marinade until well blended.
2. Place the hens in a single layer in a noncorrosive baking dish. Pour the marinade over the hens and refrigerate, covered, turning once, for 30 minutes.
3. Prepare a hot fire in a grill or preheat the broiler. Arrange the hen halves, skin side down, on a grill or a broiler pan. Grill or broil 6 inches from the heat, basting frequently with the marinade, until browned, 8 to 10 minutes. Turn skin side up and grill, basting the first 3 minutes, until the skin is browned and the juices run clear when the thigh is pricked with a fork, 8 to 10 minutes longer. Serve warm or at room temperature.

Calories: 338   Protein: 34 gm   Total Fat: 17 gm
Saturated Fat: 5 gm Cholesterol: 110 mg   Carbohydrates: 10 gm
Sodium: 103 mg

A SUPER SOURCE OF:
Phosphorus ━━━━ 23%
Niacin   ━━━━━━━━━ 53%

└─   ─┘
0%   U.S. Recommended Daily Allowance   100%

Figure your daily fat limit:
a. Figure out how many calories you consume daily.
b. Multiply the answer by .30.
c. Divide the result by 9.

Orange-Basil Cornish Hens

This dish makes wonderful summer picnic fare when basil is in season. The hens can be cooked completely ahead and eaten at room temperature. 4 SERVINGS

½ *cup orange juice*
½ *cup fresh basil leaves*
2 *tablespoons fresh lemon juice*
1 *tablespoon olive oil*
3 *garlic cloves, crushed*
1 *teaspoon grated orange zest*
½ *teaspoon salt*
¼ *teaspoon freshly ground pepper*
2 *Cornish game hens (about 1¼ pounds each), backbone removed and halved*

1. In a food processor or blender, place the orange juice, basil, lemon juice, olive oil, garlic, orange zest, salt and pepper. Puree the marinade until smooth.
2. Place the Cornish hen halves in a noncorrosive baking pan, in a single layer. Pour the marinade over the hens. Refrigerate, covered, turning once, for 30 minutes.
3. Preheat the broiler. Arrange the hen halves on the broiler pan, skin side down. Broil 6 inches from the heat, basting with the marinade until browned, 8 to 10 minutes. Turn skin side up, baste, and broil until the skin is browned and the juices run clear when the thigh is pricked with a fork, 8 to 10 minutes longer. Serve warm or at room temperature.

Calories: 326	Protein: 34 gm	Total Fat: 19 gm
Saturated Fat: 5 gm	Cholesterol: 110 mg	Carbohydrates: 3 gm
Sodium: 238 mg		

A *SUPER SOURCE OF:*
Phosphorus ━━━━━ 24%
Niacin ━━━━━━━━━━━ 54%
└─   ─┘
0%   U.S. Recommended Daily Allowance   100%

Uncooked chicken can be safely stored in the refrigerator 2 to 3 days after purchasing. Uncooked chicken can be safely stored in the freezer in freezer wrap up to 6 months.

Grilled Cornish Hens
with Pineapple-Pepper Salsa

Salsas make great "sauces" because they're simple to make, a colorful complement to the dish and usually have little or no fat.

4 SERVINGS

½ *cup unsweetened pineapple juice*
½ *cup fresh coriander leaves*
2 *tablespoons fresh lime juice*
1 *tablespoon white wine vinegar*
1 *tablespoon olive oil*
3 *garlic cloves, halved*
1 *teaspoon ground cumin*
½ *teaspoon cayenne pepper*
½ *teaspoon salt*
2 *Cornish game hens (about 1¼ pounds each), backbone removed and halved*
Pineapple-Pepper Salsa (recipe follows)

1. In a food processor or blender, combine all the ingredients except the Cornish hens and salsa. Puree the marinade until blended.

2. Place the hen halves in a single layer in a noncorrosive baking pan. Pour the marinade over the hens and refrigerate, covered, turning once, for 30 minutes.

3. Light a hot fire in a grill or preheat the broiler. Arrange the hen halves, skin side down, on the grill or broiler pan. Grill or broil 6 inches from the heat, basting frequently with the marinade until browned, 8 to 10 minutes. Turn skin side up and cook, basting the first 3 minutes, until the skin is browned and the juices run clear when the thigh is pricked with a fork, 8 to 10 minutes longer. Serve warm or at room temperature with the Pineapple-Pepper Salsa.

*P*ineapple Pepper Salsa

MAKES ABOUT 1 CUP

½ *cup finely diced fresh or canned unsweetened pineapple*
½ *cup finely diced red bell pepper*
1 *tablespoon fresh lime juice*
1 *scallion, thinly sliced*
1 *small fresh or pickled jalapeño pepper, seeded and
   minced*

In a small bowl, combine all the ingredients, stirring until blended.

Calories: 340   Protein: 35 gm   Total Fat: 19 gm
Saturated Fat: 5 gm Cholesterol: 110 mg   Carbohydrates: 6 gm
Sodium: 239 mg

A SUPER SOURCE OF:

Phosphorus ━━━━━━━ 24%
Vitamin A   ━━━━━━━ 24%
Niacin   ━━━━━━━━━━━━━ 54%
Vitamin C   ━━━━━━━━━━━━━━━━━ 74%

0%   U.S. Recommended Daily Allowance   100%

To achieve and maintain a desirable body weight, limit the
consumption of foods high in calories, fats and sugar and balance calorie intake with physical activity.

Chili-Rubbed Cornish Hens with Pumpkin Seed Sauce

This recipe, from my sister Louise, who lives in Tucson, Arizona, reflects the influence the Southwest has had on me. 4 SERVINGS

1 tablespoon Chinese chili paste with garlic
1 tablespoon distilled white vinegar
1 tablespoon orange juice
1 tablespoon chopped fresh coriander or parsley
1 teaspoon ground cinnamon
½ teaspoon salt
¼ teaspoon freshly ground pepper
2 Cornish game hens (about 1¼ pounds each), backbone removed, hens halved
Pumpkin Seed Sauce (recipe follows)

1. In a food processor or blender, combine the chili paste, vinegar, orange juice, coriander, cinnamon, salt and pepper. Puree until smooth. Rub this spice paste over the hens and refrigerate, covered, 30 minutes to 1 hour.
2. Preheat the broiler. Arrange the hens on a broiler pan, skin side down. Broil 6 inches from the heat, basting with the pan drippings, until browned, 8 to 10 minutes. Turn skin side up, baste, and broil until the skin is browned and the juices run clear when the thigh is pricked with a fork, 8 to 10 minutes longer. Serve warm or at room temperature with the Pumpkin Seed Sauce.

Pumpkin Seed Sauce

MAKES ABOUT ⅔ CUP

4 ounces fresh or canned tomatillos*
¼ cup unsalted hulled pumpkin seeds (pepitas)
2 tablespoons chopped onion
1 tablespoon chopped fresh coriander
1 small fresh or pickled jalapeño pepper, seeded and chopped
1 garlic clove, chopped
¼ teaspoon salt
¼ teaspoon freshly ground pepper
⅛ teaspoon sugar

1. In a small noncorrosive saucepan, place the fresh tomatillos with enough water to cover. Cook over medium heat until soft, 8 to 10 minutes; drain. (If using canned tomatillos, eliminate cooking and just drain.)
2. In a small skillet, toast the pumpkin seeds over medium heat, shaking the pan frequently, until browned, about 5 minutes.
3. In a food processor, grind the pumpkin seeds to a fine powder. Add the tomatillos, onion, coriander, jalapeño pepper, garlic, salt, pepper and sugar. Process until blended.
4. Transfer the mixture to a small skillet and heat over low heat just until hot, 2 to 3 minutes. (The sauce will thicken slightly as it stands. Thin with water to desired consistency.)

Calories: 342   Protein: 36 gm   Total Fat: 19 gm
Saturated Fat: 5 gm   Cholesterol: 110 mg   Carbohydrates: 6 gm
Sodium: 537 mg

A SUPER SOURCE OF:
Phosphorus   ━━━━━━━ 25%
Niacin   ━━━━━━━━━━━━━━━━ 59%
Vitamin C   ━━━━━ 20%

0%   U.S. Recommended Daily Allowance   100%

*Fresh or canned tomatillos (Mexican green tomatoes) are available in Latin American groceries, specialty food stores and the Spanish sections of some supermarkets.

Five-Spice Cornish Hens

4 SERVINGS

2 *tablespoons reduced-sodium soy sauce*
2 *tablespoons rice wine vinegar*
2 *tablespoons chopped scallions*
2 *teaspoons Chinese five-spice powder**
2 *teaspoons Asian sesame oil*
1 *teaspoon sugar*
2 *garlic cloves, crushed*
2 *Cornish game hens (about 1¼ pounds each), backbone removed, hens halved*

1. In a noncorrosive baking dish, combine the soy sauce, vinegar, scallions, five-spice powder, sesame oil, sugar and garlic. Stir to blend. Add the hen halves and refrigerate, covered, turning once, for 30 minutes.
2. Preheat the broiler. Arrange the hen halves, skin side down, on the broiler pan. Broil 6 inches from the heat, basting with the marinade, until browned, 8 to 10 minutes. Turn skin side up and broil, basting the first 3 minutes, until the skin is browned and the juices run clear when the thigh is pricked with a fork, 8 to 10 minutes longer. Serve warm or at room temperature.

Calories: 315   Protein: 34 gm   Total Fat: 18 gm
Saturated Fat: 5 gm   Cholesterol: 110 mg   Carbohydrates: 1 gm
Sodium: 253 mg

A SUPER SOURCE OF:
Phosphorus ▬▬▬▬ 23%
Niacin   ▬▬▬▬▬▬▬▬ 54%

0%   U.S. Recommended Daily Allowance   100%

*Five-spice powder is available in Oriental markets and the spice section of some supermarkets.

Gingery Game Hens

Three types of ginger are used in the marinade: ground ginger, fresh ginger and stem ginger in syrup. 4 SERVINGS

*2 tablespoons stem ginger, finely chopped, plus ¼ cup
  ginger syrup from the jar*
2 tablespoons fresh lemon juice
1 tablespoon reduced-sodium soy sauce
1 tablespoon light brown sugar
2 teaspoons grated fresh ginger
½ teaspoon ground ginger
*2 Cornish game hens (about 1¼ pounds each), backbone
  removed and halved*

1. In a baking dish, combine the chopped stem ginger, ginger syrup, lemon juice, soy sauce, brown sugar, fresh ginger and ground ginger. Stir to blend. Add the hen halves and refrigerate, covered, turning once, for 30 minutes.

2. Preheat the broiler. Arrange the hen halves, skin side down, on a broiler pan. Broil 6 inches from the heat, basting with the marinade, until browned, 8 to 10 minutes. Turn skin side up and broil, basting the first 3 minutes, until the skin is browned and the juices run clear when the thigh is pricked with a fork, 8 to 10 minutes longer. Serve warm or at room temperature.

Calories: 383	Protein: 34 gm	Total Fat: 17 gm
Saturated Fat: 5 gm	Cholesterol: 110 mg	Carbohydrates: 22 gm
Sodium: 255 mg		

A SUPER SOURCE OF:

Phosphorus ━━━━━━ 24%
Niacin ━━━━━━━━━━━━ 54%

0%   U.S. Recommended Daily Allowance   100%

Maximize your Microwave

With a microwave oven in 75 percent of all households today, it's not just a food fad, but a fact of life. The microwave does not replace a conventional oven, stove top or toaster, but it does add another method of cooking. It's important to learn how to make the best use of the microwave beyond reheating and defrosting foods.

Microwaving is a quick and convenient timesaver that ensures even cooking. It's perfect for keeping boneless, skinless chicken breasts tender, moist and juicy, as with Chicken Cheese Vegetable Bundles, which are wrapped in dampened paper towels, seal in all the flavor and juices and cook in just 2½ minutes in the microwave.

When cooked quickly and paired with chicken, vegetables such as potatoes, spaghetti squash or artichokes make perfect partners for everyday family dinners.

An added benefit of microwave cooking is a healthy one. It requires little fat, and there's little loss of nutrients when food is cooked so quickly.

Note: These recipes were tested in a 600- to 700-watt microwave oven.

Confetti Stuffed Peppers

4 SERVINGS

1 ounce pine nuts
4 large red, green and/or yellow bell peppers
1 teaspoon olive oil
½ cup finely chopped onion
1 garlic clove, minced
½ pound ground chicken
½ cup cooked long-grain white rice
¼ cup frozen peas, defrosted
1 tablespoon chopped fresh basil or parsley
½ teaspoon salt
¼ teaspoon freshly ground pepper
¼ cup canned tomato puree
2 tablespoons grated Parmesan cheese

1. Spread the pine nuts evenly on a paper plate or microwave-safe paper towel. Toast on High, stirring once, until lightly browned, 2 to 4 minutes; set aside.

2. Cut ½ inch from the stem end of the peppers. Discard the stem and finely chop the ends; set aside. Remove the ribs and seeds from the peppers, leaving them intact.

3. Place the peppers, cut side down, with 2 tablespoons water in a 2-quart microwave-safe dish. Cover with microwave-safe plastic wrap and cook on High until the peppers are crisp-tender, 2 minutes. Let cool while preparing the filling.

4. In a 1-quart microwave safe dish, combine the olive oil, onion and garlic. Cover and cook on High 2 minutes. Add the ground chicken and the reserved chopped pepper tops and cook, tightly covered, breaking up the chicken with the back of a spoon halfway through, until the chicken is no longer pink, about 5 minutes. Remove from the oven and stir in the rice, peas, pine nuts, basil, salt and pepper. Spoon the filling into the peppers. Spoon 1 tablespoon tomato puree over the top of each pepper.

5. Place the peppers back in the microwave-safe dish and cover with wax paper. Cook on Medium until heated through, 5 to 7 minutes. Let stand 3 minutes. Sprinkle ½ tablespoon Parmesan cheese over each pepper.

Calories: 226	Protein: 15 gm	Total Fat: 11 gm
Saturated Fat: 3 gm	Cholesterol: 49 mg	Carbohydrates: 18 gm
Sodium: 443 mg		

A SUPER SOURCE OF:

Iron	▬▬▬ 22%
Vitamin A	▬▬▬▬▬▬▬▬▬▬▬▬▬▬▬▬▬ 100%
Vitamin C	▬▬▬▬▬▬▬▬▬▬▬▬▬▬▬▬▬ 100%

0%   U.S. Recommended Daily Allowance   100%

Chinese Chicken, Mushrooms and Spinach in Garlic Sauce

4 SERVINGS

1 pound skinless, boneless chicken breasts
2 tablespoons rice wine or dry sherry
1 tablespoon minced fresh ginger
1 tablespoon cornstarch
1 tablespoon reduced-sodium soy sauce
1 teaspoon Asian sesame oil
1/2 teaspoon sugar
1/4 teaspoon crushed hot pepper flakes
3 garlic cloves, minced
2 teaspoons peanut oil
1 red bell pepper, cut into 1/2-inch dice
2 scallions, sliced
10 ounces fresh spinach, rinsed, well drained and stemmed
1/4 cup no-salt chicken broth
1 can (15 ounces) straw mushrooms, rinsed and drained

1. Place the chicken between 2 pieces of plastic wrap. Pound gently to flatten to an even 1/8-inch thickness.
2. In a large shallow bowl, whisk together the rice wine, ginger, cornstarch, soy sauce, sesame oil, sugar, hot pepper and garlic. Add the chicken and toss to coat. Marinate 30 minutes.
3. In a 2½- to 3-quart microwave-safe dish, heat the oil, uncovered, on High 2 minutes. Add the chicken and marinade, cover and cook on High 1 minute. Stir and cook, covered, on High 1 minute longer. Add the bell pepper and scallions, cover and cook on High 1 minute. Add the spinach and chicken broth and cook, covered, on High 2 minutes. Add the mushrooms, stir and cook, covered, on High 1 minute. Let stand, covered, 3 to 5 minutes before serving. Serve hot with cooked brown rice.

Calories: 218	Protein: 30 gm	Total Fat: 5 gm
Saturated Fat: 1 gm	Cholesterol: 66 mg	Carbohydrates: 12 gm
Sodium: 476 mg		

A SUPER SOURCE OF:

Phosphorus	29%
Vitamin A	98%
Niacin	68%
Vitamin C	92%

0%   U.S. Recommended Daily Allowance   100%

Spaghetti Squash with Chunky Chicken Tomato Sauce

4 SERVINGS

1 large spaghetti squash (about 4 pounds)
2 teaspoons olive oil
½ cup chopped onion
1 small green bell pepper, chopped
1 garlic clove, minced
1 pound ground chicken
1 can (28 ounces) Italian peeled tomatoes, drained and chopped
1 teaspoon oregano
¼ teaspoon salt
¼ teaspoon freshly ground pepper
2 tablespoons chopped parsley
¼ cup grated Parmesan cheese

1. Pierce the spaghetti squash deeply several times with a long-tined fork. Place on a 9-inch microwave-safe dish and cook on High until the squash feels slightly soft, about 15 minutes. Wrap in a kitchen towel and let stand while preparing the sauce.
2. In a 3-quart microwave-safe dish, combine the olive oil, onion, bell pepper and garlic. Cover with microwave-safe plastic wrap and cook on High, stirring once, 3 to 5 minutes. Add the chicken, spreading evenly in the dish, and cook, covered, on High, breaking up any lumps with the back of a spoon halfway through, 5 to 6 minutes. Add the tomatoes, oregano, salt and pepper. Cook on High, stirring once, 10 minutes. Let stand, covered, 5 minutes.
3. Using oven mitts, cut the squash in half. Remove the seeds, then pull the squash strands into a large bowl with a fork.
4. Divide the squash among 4 serving plates. Spoon the sauce over the squash. Sprinkle the parsley and Parmesan cheese on top.

Calories: 377	Protein: 26 gm	Total Fat: 16 gm
Saturated Fat: 4 gm	Cholesterol: 98 mg	Carbohydrates: 34 gm
Sodium: 700 mg		

A SUPER SOURCE OF:

Calcium	▬▬▬	24%
Phosphorus	▬▬▬	26%
Iron	▬▬▬	28%
Vitamin A	▬▬▬▬	35%
Riboflavin	▬▬	22%
Niacin	▬▬▬▬▬	47%
Vitamin C	▬▬▬▬▬▬▬▬▬▬	100%

0%   U.S. Recommended Daily Allowance   100%

Sweet and Sour Stuffed Cabbage

MAKES 4 SERVINGS

1 small head of cabbage (about 1 pound)
¼ cup long-grain white rice
1 teaspoon vegetable oil
½ cup chopped onion
1 garlic clove, minced
½ pound ground chicken
½ cup chopped pitted prunes or raisins
1 large egg, lightly beaten
2 teaspoons caraway seeds
¾ teaspoon salt
½ teaspoon freshly ground pepper
1 cup canned tomato puree
2 tablespoons dark brown sugar
2 tablespoons cider vinegar

1. Cut the core away from the cabbage. Finely chop the core and
set aside.
2. Place the whole cabbage and 2 tablespoons water in a 2-quart
microwave-safe dish. Cover tightly with microwave-safe plastic wrap
and cook on High until the leaves are softened, 5 to 8 minutes.
Detach 8 large leaves. Remove the remaining cabbage for another
use.
3. In the same 2-quart microwave-safe dish, combine the rice and
½ cup water and cook, covered with plastic wrap, on High until
boiling, about 2 minutes. Cook on Medium until most of the water
is absorbed, 5 to 7 minutes. Stir and let stand, covered, 5 minutes.
4. In a 2-quart microwave-safe dish, combine the oil, onion and
garlic. Cook, covered with microwave-safe plastic wrap, on High
until softened, 2 to 3 minutes. Add the reserved chopped cabbage
core and cook, covered, on High until crisp-tender, about 5
minutes. Remove from the microwave. Add the cooked rice, ground
chicken, chopped prunes, egg, caraway seeds, salt and pepper. Stir
to blend well.
5. With a sharp knife, cut away the thick central ribs from the 8
cabbage leaves. Place about ¼ cup of the stuffing on each leaf. Roll
up each leaf from the stem, tucking in the sides to make a neat
package; secure with a toothpick.

6. In a 2-quart microwave-safe dish, combine the tomato puree, brown sugar and vinegar; stir until well blended. Place the stuffed cabbage rolls, seam side down, in the sauce. Tightly cover with microwave-safe plastic wrap and cook on High 10 minutes. Cook on Medium 20 minutes. Let stand, covered, 10 minutes before serving.

Calories: 298   Protein: 16 gm   Total Fat: 8 gm
Saturated Fat: 2 gm   Cholesterol: 100 mg   Carbohydrates: 44 gm
Sodium: 748 mg

A SUPER SOURCE OF:
Iron   ▬▬▬ 23%
Vitamin A   ▬▬▬▬ 31%
Niacin   ▬▬ 23%
Vitamin C   ▬▬▬▬▬▬▬▬▬▬▬▬▬▬▬▬ 100%

0%   U.S. Recommended Daily Allowance   100%

The total grams of fat in a 2-ounce cooked ground beef patty is three times greater than in 2 ounces of skinless roasted chicken.

Stuffed Artichokes with Chicken, Olives and Pine Nuts

Artichokes cook so quickly in the microwave—these 4 take only 11 minutes—you'll be encouraged to prepare them all the time.

4 SERVINGS

2 ounces pine nuts (about ½ cup)
4 large artichokes
½ lemon
¾ cup no-salt chicken broth
1 teaspoon olive oil
1 large onion, chopped (about 1 cup)
1 garlic clove, minced
1 cup diced smoked chicken (about 4 ounces)
¼ cup plain dry bread crumbs
¼ cup grated Parmesan cheese
3 tablespoons pitted Calamata olives, chopped
½ teaspoon dried thyme leaves
¼ teaspoon freshly ground pepper

1. Spread the pine nuts evenly on a paper plate or microwave-safe paper towel. Toast on High, until lightly browned, 2 to 4 minutes, stirring once; set aside.
2. Cut off the artichoke stems. Cut about 1½ inches from the tops of the artichokes. Snip off the points of the outer leaves. Rub the artichokes with the cut side of the lemon.
3. Place the artichokes in a 2½-quart microwave-safe dish. Pour ¼ cup of the chicken broth into the bottom of the dish. Cover tightly with microwave-safe plastic wrap and cook on High until the bottoms are tender when pierced with the tip of a knife, about 11 minutes. Let stand, covered, 3 minutes; drain.
4. When cool enough to handle, pull out the center leaves. With a spoon or melon baller, remove the center choke.

5. In the same microwave-safe dish, cook the oil, onion and garlic, uncovered, on High, 3 minutes. Add the chicken, bread crumbs, cheese, olives, pine nuts, thyme, pepper and ¼ cup of the chicken broth. Stir until well blended. Spoon the mixture into the center of the artichokes and in between the leaves. Pour the remaining ¼ cup chicken broth into the same dish. Place the artichokes in the dish stem side down. Cover tightly with microwave-safe plastic wrap and cook on High until heated through, about 4 minutes.

Calories: 298	Protein: 19 gm	Total Fat: 15 gm
Saturated Fat: 3 gm	Cholesterol: 29 mg	Carbohydrates: 28 gm
Sodium: 748 mg		

A SUPER SOURCE OF:

Phosphorous	▬▬▬▬▬	28%
Iron	▬▬▬▬	26%
Niacin	▬▬▬	23%
Vitamin C	▬▬▬▬▬▬	42%

0%   U.S. Recommended Daily Allowance   100%

Chicken Cheese Vegetable Bundles

2 SERVINGS

4 sun-dried tomatoes
1 tablespoon balsamic vinegar
2 teaspoons olive oil
2 teaspoons Dijon mustard
½ teaspoon oregano
¼ teaspoon salt
¼ teaspoon freshly ground pepper
½ pound skinless, boneless chicken breasts, cut into ½-inch
  diagonal strips
½ cup thin strips of zucchini
½ cup thin strips yellow bell pepper
¼ cup shredded fresh basil
1 scallion, thinly sliced
1 ounce goat cheese, crumbled

1. Place the sun-dried tomatoes and 2 tablespoons water in a 1-cup microwave-safe measuring cup. Cover tightly and heat on High until softened, 30 to 45 seconds. Let stand, covered, for 1 minute.
2. In a small bowl, whisk together the vinegar, olive oil, mustard, oregano, salt and pepper.
3. Place the chicken in a bowl. In another bowl, combine the zucchini, bell pepper, sun-dried tomatoes, basil and scallion. Pour half the dressing over the chicken; toss to coat. Add the remaining dressing to the vegetables and toss to coat.
4. Layer 3 sheets of microwave-safe paper towels together and soak thoroughly with tap water. Wring out very lightly and smooth. Place half the vegetables in the center of the wet paper towels. Arrange half the chicken on top of the vegetables. Sprinkle half the goat cheese on top. Bring up the corners of the towels and twist tightly together to enclose the chicken and vegetables. Repeat with the remaining vegetables, chicken and goat cheese.
5. Place the bundles on a microwave-safe plate and cook on High until the chicken is just cooked through and the vegetables are crisp-tender, 2 to 2½ minutes.

Calories: 276	Protein: 31 gm	Total Fat: 11 gm
Saturated Fat: 1 gm	Cholesterol: 79 mg	Carbohydrates: 14 gm
Sodium: 598 mg		

A *SUPER SOURCE OF:*

Vitamin A	████████████████ 57%	
Niacin	█████████████████ 71%	
Vitamin C	████████████████████████ 100%	

0%   U.S. Recommended Daily Allowance   100%

Sweet Potatoes Stuffed with Smoked Chicken

Smoked chicken, toasted pecans and spiced honey make up this flavorful filling for the sweet potatoes. 4 SERVINGS

4 large sweet potatoes (about 8 ounces each)
½ cup shelled pecans
½ pound smoked chicken, diced (about 1 cup)
2 tablespoons chopped fresh chives
2 tablespoons honey
1 tablespoon light brown sugar
½ teaspoon ground ginger
¼ teaspoon ground cinnamon
¼ teaspoon salt
¼ teaspoon freshly ground pepper

1. Pierce the sweet potato skins in several places with a fork. Place the sweet potatoes 1 inch apart on a microwave-safe paper towel. Cook, uncovered, on High, turning once, until tender, 10 to 12 minutes. Let stand while preparing the filling.
2. Spread the pecans evenly on a paper plate or microwave-safe paper towel. Toast on High until lightly browned, 2 to 2½ minutes, stirring once.
3. In a small bowl, combine the smoked chicken, chives, honey, brown sugar, ginger, cinnamon and pecans. Stir until well blended.
4. Scoop out the sweet potatoes, leaving a ¼-inch shell. In a large bowl, mash the sweet potatoes. Add the chicken mixture and the salt and pepper. Stir until well blended. Spoon back into the shells, dividing evenly. Place the potatoes on a microwave-safe plate and cook, uncovered, on High until hot, 3 to 4 minutes.

Calories: 416	Protein: 20 gm	Total Fat: 14 gm
Saturated Fat: 2 gm	Cholesterol: 50 mg	Carbohydrates: 54 gm
Sodium: 709 mg		

A SUPER SOURCE OF:
Riboflavin ━━━━━ 21%
Niacin ━━━━━━━ 32%
Vitamin C ━━━━━━━━━━━━━━ 64%

0%   U.S. Recommended Daily Allowance   100%

SPEEDY SAUTÉS AND STIR-FRYS

The key to successful sautéing and stir-frying is preparing all the ingredients beforehand, quick cooking over high heat, which results in even cooking, and using the correct type of skillet. To prevent foods from sticking when using little or no fat, a good nonstick skillet or wok is essential.

The recipes in this chapter live up to its title; most take 15 minutes or less to cook. They can be dressed up or down depending on what garnishes and flavorings are added to the pan. Spicy Chicken and Chips, with its oven-browned potato slices, makes everyday fare the entire family will love. Lemon Chicken with Roasted Asparagus is an elegant, beautifully presented dish that can dress up a dinner table while keeping calories down. Dishes like Chicken au Poivre with Carrot Puree, Chinese Vegetable Chicken Stir-Fry and Venetian-Style Chicken with Raisins and Pine Nuts take you around the world in no time. While all the recipes in this chapter were designed to make four servings, when there are only two of you for dinner, they can be halved easily.

Deviled Chicken Breasts

These honey mustard–coated chicken breasts can be made in just 15 minutes. 4 SERVINGS

2 tablespoons honey
2 tablespoons coarse grainy mustard
1 tablespoon tarragon wine vinegar
2 teaspoons Dijon mustard
½ cup plain dry bread crumbs
½ teaspoon tarragon, crumbled
½ teaspoon salt
½ teaspoon freshly ground pepper
4 skinless, boneless chicken breast halves (4 ounces each)
2 teaspoons olive oil

1. In a large shallow bowl, combine the honey, grainy mustard, wine vinegar and Dijon mustard. Stir to blend.
2. On a flat plate, combine the bread crumbs, tarragon, salt and pepper.
3. Dip the chicken in the mustard mixture to coat completely. Then dredge in the seasoned bread crumbs.
4. In a large nonstick skillet, heat the oil over medium heat. Add the chicken and cook, turning once, until golden brown outside and white throughout but still juicy, 5 to 7 minutes.

Calories: 238	Protein: 28 gm	Total Fat: 5 gm
Saturated Fat: 1 gm	Cholesterol: 66 mg	Carbohydrates: 19 gm
Sodium: 590 mg		

A *SUPER SOURCE OF:*

Phosphorus ▬▬▬▬ 25%
Niacin ▬▬▬▬▬▬▬▬▬▬ 67%

0%   U.S. Recommended Daily Allowance   100%

When buying chicken, make sure it smells fresh, is not discolored, and check package date. Make sure that the skin is unblemished and without any bruises.

Chicken Milanese Salad

4 SERVINGS

4 skinless, boneless chicken breast halves (4 ounces each)
1 large egg
²⁄₃ cup plain dry bread crumbs
2 tablespoons grated Parmesan cheese
¾ teaspoon salt
½ teaspoon freshly ground pepper
1 garlic clove, halved
2 tablespoons red wine vinegar
2 teaspoons extra-virgin olive oil
1 bunch arugula or watercress
1 small red onion, sliced
1 large Belgian endive, leaves separated and halved
   lengthwise
½ pound fresh plum tomatoes, cut into ½-inch dice (about
   1 cup)

1. Place each piece of chicken between 2 pieces of plastic wrap. Pound gently to flatten each piece to an even ¼-inch thickness.
2. In a shallow bowl, beat the egg with 1 tablespoon water.
3. On a large flat plate, combine the bread crumbs, Parmesan cheese, ½ teaspoon of the salt and ¼ teaspoon of the pepper.
3. Dip the chicken into the beaten egg, then coat with the bread crumb mixture.
4. Coat a large nonstick skillet with vegetable cooking spray and heat over medium heat. Add the chicken and cook, turning once, until golden brown outside and white throughout, but still juicy, 5 to 6 minutes.
5. Meanwhile, rub a medium bowl with the cut side of garlic. Add the vinegar, oil, remaining ½ teaspoon salt and ¼ teaspoon pepper. Whisk to blend. Add the arugula, onion, endive and tomatoes. Toss gently to coat.
6. Place the warm chicken on 4 serving plates and top with the salad.

Calories: 266   Protein: 33   Total Fat: 7 gm
Saturated Fat: 2 gm   Cholesterol: 122 mg Carbohydrates: 17 gm
Sodium: 695 mg

A SUPER SOURCE OF:
Phosphorus   ━━━━━━━━ 34%
Vitamin A   ━━━━━━━━━━━━ 55%
Niacin   ━━━━━━━━━━━━━━━ 70%
Vitamin C   ━━━━━━━━━━━ 54%

└─   ─┘
  0%   U.S. Recommended Daily Allowance   100%

Chicken au Poivre with Carrot Puree

The sweetness of the carrots in this rich tasting but low-fat puree is a great counterpoint to these peppery chicken breasts. 4 SERVINGS

½ pound carrots, peeled and thickly sliced
2 tablespoons buttermilk
½ teaspoon salt
¼ teaspoon freshly ground pepper
Pinch of nutmeg
1 tablespoon whole peppercorns
4 skinless, boneless chicken breast halves (4 ounces each)

1. In a large saucepan, place the carrots with enough water to cover. Heat over medium heat to boiling. Cook, covered, until tender, 18 to 20 minutes; drain.
2. In a food processor or blender, combine the carrots, buttermilk, ¼ teaspoon of the salt, the pepper and the nutmeg. Puree until smooth. (The puree can be covered and refrigerated several hours or overnight. Before serving, heat in a small heavy saucepan, over low heat, stirring constantly.)
3. Place the peppercorns in a small heavy plastic bag and pound with the flat side of a cleaver or the bottom of a heavy skillet until cracked to medium-fine.
4. Season the chicken with the remaining ¼ teaspoon salt and the cracked pepper.
5. Coat a large nonstick skillet with vegetable cooking spray and heat over medium heat. Add the chicken and cook, turning once, until browned outside and white throughout, but still juicy, 5 to 7 minutes. Serve immediately, with the carrot puree on the side.

Calories: 156	Protein: 27 gm	Total Fat: 2 gm
Saturated Fat: 0 gm	Cholesterol: 66 mg	Carbohydrates: 7 gm
Sodium: 374 mg		

A SUPER SOURCE OF:

Phosphorus ━━━━━ 25%
Vitamin A ━━━━━━━━━━━━━━━━━━━━━━━ 100%
Niacin ━━━━━━━━━━━━━━━━━ 66%

0%   U.S. Recommended Daily Allowance   100%

Chinese Vegetable Chicken Stir-Fry

4 SERVINGS

2 tablespoons vegetable oil
1 tablespoon reduced-sodium soy sauce
2 teaspoons cornstarch
¼ teaspoon crushed hot pepper flakes
1 large egg white
1 pound skinless, boneless chicken breasts, cut into ¼-inch
    strips
4 ounces snow peas, trimmed
1 red bell pepper, cut into ¼-inch strips
4 ounces unsalted roasted cashews (1 cup)
1 tablespoon minced fresh ginger
1 garlic clove, minced
1 can (15 ounces) baby corn, rinsed and drained
1 can (15 ounces) straw mushrooms, rinsed and drained

1. In a large bowl, whisk together 1 tablespoon of the oil, the soy sauce, cornstarch, hot pepper flakes and egg white. Add the chicken and stir to coat completely. Refrigerate, covered, 30 minutes.
2. In a large nonstick skillet or wok, heat the remaining 1 tablespoon oil over medium-high heat. Add the snow peas and bell pepper and cook, stirring constantly, until crisp-tender, 2 minutes; transfer with a slotted spoon to a bowl.
3. Add the cashews to the skillet and cook, stirring constantly, 1 minute; transfer with a slotted spoon to the same bowl. Add the ginger and garlic to the skillet and cook, stirring constantly, 1 minute. Add the chicken and cook, stirring constantly, until white throughout, about 3 minutes. Add the corn, mushrooms and reserved vegetables and cook, stirring constantly, until hot, 2 minutes. Serve with steamed rice.

Calories: 454	Protein: 36 gm	Total Fat: 22 gm
Saturated Fat: 4 gm	Cholesterol: 66 mg	Carbohydrates: 31 gm
Sodium: 450 mg		

A SUPER SOURCE OF:

Phosphorus	━━━━━━━	42%
Iron	━━━━━	26%
Vitamin A	━━━━	25%
Niacin	━━━━━━━━━━━	68%
Vitamin C	━━━━━━━━━━━━━	90%

0%	U.S. Recommended Daily Allowance	100%

Venetian-Style Chicken with Raisins and Pine Nuts

4 SERVINGS

¼ cup golden raisins
1 ounce pine nuts
2 teaspoons olive oil
2 large onions, sliced
4 skinless, boneless chicken breast halves (4 ounces each)
½ teaspoon salt
½ teaspoon freshly ground pepper
¼ cup balsamic vinegar

1. Put the raisins in a small bowl and add hot water to cover. Let stand 30 minutes.
2. In a small skillet, toast the pine nuts over medium heat, shaking the pan frequently, until browned, about 5 minutes; set aside.
3. In a large nonstick skillet, heat the oil over medium heat. Add the onions and cook, stirring occasionally, until golden brown, 7 to 10 minutes. Transfer to a large plate. Cover with foil to keep warm.
4. Coat the same skillet with vegetable cooking spray and heat over medium heat. Season the chicken with the salt and pepper. Add the chicken and cook, turning once, until browned outside and white throughout, but still juicy, 5 to 7 minutes. Transfer the chicken to the plate with the onions.
5. Drain the raisins. Add to the same skillet along with the vinegar. Heat to boiling and cook 1 minute. Pour over the chicken and onion. Sprinkle with pine nuts and serve.

Calories: 240	Protein: 29 gm	Total Fat: 8 gm
Saturated Fat: 1 gm	Cholesterol: 66 mg	Carbohydrates: 15 gm
Sodium: 350 mg		

A SUPER SOURCE OF:
Phosphorus ▬▬▬▬ 29%
Niacin ▬▬▬▬▬▬▬▬▬ 66%

0%   U.S. Recommended Daily Allowance   100%

The USDA's Meat and Poultry Hotline number is 1-800-535-4555. Professional home economists will answer any questions about proper handling of meat and poultry, what's safe to eat, and about labeling.

Chicken with Lemon Caper Sauce

Another great 15-minute dinner that can be put together right after work. Serve with fluffy rice and crunchy sugar snap peas or green beans. 4 SERVINGS

¼ cup all-purpose flour
½ teaspoon salt
½ teaspoon freshly ground pepper
4 skinless, boneless chicken breast halves (4 ounces each)
½ cup no-salt chicken broth
2 tablespoons finely chopped watercress
2 tablespoons minced shallots
2 tablespoons capers, rinsed and drained
2 teaspoons Dijon mustard
2 teaspoons fresh lemon juice
1 teaspoon grated lemon zest
Watercress sprigs, for garnish

1. On a large flat plate, combine the flour, salt and pepper. Dust the chicken with the seasoned flour to coat completely. Shake off any excess.
2. Coat a large nonstick skillet with vegetable cooking spray and heat over medium heat. Add the chicken and cook, turning once, until browned outside and white throughout but still juicy, 5 to 7 minutes. Remove from the skillet; cover with foil to keep warm.
3. Add the chicken broth to the skillet and heat to boiling, scraping up any browned bits from the bottom of the pan. Boil for 2 minutes. Add the chopped watercress, shallots, capers, mustard, lemon juice and lemon zest. Cook 2 minutes. Pour the sauce over the chicken and garnish with sprigs of watercress.

Calories: 167	Protein: 27 gm	Total Fat: 2 gm
Saturated Fat: 0 gm	Cholesterol: 66 mg	Carbohydrates: 8 gm
Sodium: 540 mg		

A SUPER SOURCE OF:
Phosphorus ▬▬▬ 24%
Niacin ▬▬▬▬▬▬▬▬▬ 67%

0%   U.S. Recommended Daily Allowance   100%

Spicy Chicken and Chips

A take-off on fish and chips. While the chips bake in the oven, prepare the chicken and quickly cook just before the chips are done. 4 SERVINGS

1½ pounds all-purpose potatoes, cut into ⅛-inch slices
1 teaspoon salt
1 teaspoon freshly ground pepper
¼ cup all-purpose flour
½ teaspoon cayenne pepper
½ teaspoon ground cumin
1 pound skinless, boneless chicken breasts, cut diagonally
   into 1-inch strips
1 tablespoon fresh lime juice
2 teaspoons vegetable oil

1. Preheat the oven to 400 degrees. Coat a baking sheet with vegetable cooking spray. Arrange the potato slices in a single layer on the sheet. Season with ½ teaspoon of the salt and ½ teaspoon of the black pepper. Bake until crisp and browned, 35 to 40 minutes.

2. Meanwhile, on a large flat plate, combine the flour, cayenne, cumin, remaining ½ teaspoon salt and ½ teaspoon black pepper. Stir to blend.

3. In a medium bowl, toss the chicken with the lime juice, then dust with the seasoned flour.

4. In a large nonstick skillet, heat the oil over medium heat. Add the chicken and cook, stirring frequently, until browned, 5 to 7 minutes. Serve hot with the chips.

Calories: 306	Protein: 31 gm	Total Fat: 4 gm
Saturated Fat: 1 gm	Cholesterol: 66 mg	Carbohydrates: 35 gm
Sodium: 637 mg		

A SUPER SOURCE OF:

Phosphorus   ━━━━━━━━ 31%
Iron   ━━━━━ 21%
Niacin   ━━━━━━━━━━━━━━━━━━━ 78%
Vitamin C   ━━━━━━━━━━━━━ 54%

0%   U.S. Recommended Daily Allowance   100%

After handling raw chicken, wash your hands and clean all work surfaces that the chicken has touched because they can harbor bacteria. This includes knives and any other work utensils.

Rosemary Chicken and Apples

4 SERVINGS

2 tablespoons all-purpose flour
1/4 teaspoon salt
1/4 teaspoon freshly ground pepper
4 skinless, boneless chicken breast halves (4 ounces each)
2 teaspoons olive oil
4 large shallots, finely chopped
1 garlic clove, minced
1 teaspoon chopped fresh rosemary or 1/2 teaspoon dried
2 Golden Delicious apples, peeled and sliced
2 teaspoons fresh lemon juice
1 cup apple cider

1. On a flat plate, combine the flour, salt and pepper. Coat the chicken with the seasoned flour; shake off any excess.

2. Coat a large nonstick skillet with vegetable cooking spray and heat over medium heat. Add the chicken and cook, turning once, until browned outside and white throughout but still juicy, 5 to 7 minutes. Remove from the skillet; keep warm.

3. In the same skillet, heat the oil over medium heat. Add the shallots, garlic and rosemary. Cook until the shallots are softened, 2 to 3 minutes. Add the apples and lemon juice and cook until the apples are softened, 5 to 7 minutes.

4. Add the cider, increase the heat to medium-high and cook until the liquid is slightly reduced, 2 to 3 minutes. Pour the apples and their liquid over the chicken.

Calories: 236   Protein: 27 gm   Total Fat: 4 gm
Saturated Fat: 1 gm   Cholesterol: 66 mg   Carbohydrates: 22 gm
Sodium: 212 mg

A SUPER SOURCE OF:
Phosphorus ━━━━━ 24%
Niacin   ━━━━━━━━━━━━━━━ 65%
Vitamin C   ━━━━━━━━━━━━ 54%

0%   U.S. Recommended Daily Allowance   100%

Lemon Chicken with Roasted Asparagus

Here is a quick but sophisticated way to dress up everyday chicken, especially in the spring when asparagus is at its peak.

4 SERVINGS

4 skinless, boneless chicken breast halves (4 ounces each)
1 tablespoon fresh lemon juice
1 teaspoon salt
½ teaspoon freshly ground pepper
½ teaspoon grated lemon zest
¾ pound fresh asparagus, trimmed
1 tablespoon olive oil
2 tablespoons seasoned dry bread crumbs
4 thin slices low-fat turkey ham (about 1 ounce)
Thin lemon slices, for garnish

1. Preheat the oven to 500 degrees. In a medium bowl, combine the chicken, lemon juice, ½ teaspoon of the salt, ¼ teaspoon of the pepper and the lemon zest. Toss to mix.
2. Place the asparagus in a single layer on a baking sheet. Sprinkle the olive oil over the asparagus and season with the remaining ½ teaspoon salt and ¼ teaspoon pepper. Roast until tender, shaking the pan occasionally, 8 to 10 minutes.
3. Meanwhile, on a large flat plate, coat the chicken with the seasoned bread crumbs.
4. Coat a large nonstick skillet with vegetable cooking spray and heat over medium-high heat. Add the chicken and cook, turning once, until golden brown outside and white throughout, but still juicy, 5 to 7 minutes.
5. Place the chicken on a serving platter. Divide the asparagus into 4 bundles. Wrap each bundle with a slice of the turkey ham and place on top of the chicken. Garnish with lemon slices.

Calories: 191	Protein: 29 gm	Total Fat: 6 gm
Saturated Fat: 1 gm	Cholesterol: 66 mg	Carbohydrates: 5 gm
Sodium: 795 mg		

A SUPER SOURCE OF:

Phosphorus	▬▬▬▬	27%
Niacin	▬▬▬▬▬▬▬▬▬▬	68%
Vitamin C	▬▬▬▬▬	31%

0%   U.S. Recommended Daily Allowance   100%

Chicken Cutlets with Tarragon Mustard Sauce

The combination of smooth Dijon and coarse grainy mustard is what gives this sauce its pleasing bite. 4 SERVINGS

4 skinless, boneless chicken breast halves (4 ounces each)
¼ cup all-purpose flour
½ teaspoon salt
¼ teaspoon freshly ground pepper
2 teaspoons olive oil
½ cup no-salt chicken broth
1 tablespoon chopped fresh chives
2 teaspoons chopped fresh tarragon or 1 teaspoon dried
2 teaspoons Dijon mustard
1 teaspoon coarse grainy mustard

1. Place each piece of chicken between 2 pieces of plastic wrap. Pound gently to flatten each piece to an even ¼-inch thickness.
2. On a large flat plate, combine the flour, salt and pepper. Dust the chicken with the seasoned flour to coat completely. Shake off any excess.
3. In a large nonstick skillet, heat the oil over medium heat. Add the chicken and cook, turning once, until browned outside and white throughout, but still juicy, 5 to 6 minutes. Remove from the skillet; cover with foil to keep warm.
4. Add the chicken broth to the skillet and heat to boiling. Boil for 2 minutes. Stir in the chives, tarragon, Dijon mustard and grainy mustard. Cook 2 minutes. Pour the sauce over the chicken and serve.

Calories: 183	Protein: 27 gm	Total Fat: 4 gm
Saturated Fat: 1 gm	Cholesterol: 66 mg	Carbohydrates: 7 gm
Sodium: 442 mg		

A SUPER SOURCE OF:

Phosphorus ━━━━━━ 23%
Niacin ━━━━━━━━━━━━━━━━ 67%

0%   U.S. Recommended Daily Allowance   100%

Substitute polyunsaturated fats (corn and safflower oil) and monounsaturated fats (canola and olive oil) for saturated fats (butter, lard, cream, cocoa butter, coconut and palm oils).

Chicken with Mushroom-Shallot Ragout

Although low in calories, the combination of different mushrooms—button and shiitake—gives this dish its rich meaty flavor and character. 4 SERVINGS

4 skinless, boneless chicken breast halves (4 ounces each)
1 teaspoon salt
½ teaspoon freshly ground pepper
2 teaspoons olive oil
¼ cup chopped shallots or scallion bulbs
1 pound fresh mushrooms, thickly sliced
½ pound fresh shiitake mushrooms, stemmed, wiped clean and thickly cut
½ cup no-salt chicken broth
2 teaspoons fresh lemon juice
½ teaspoon dried thyme leaves

1. Place each piece of chicken between 2 pieces of plastic wrap. Pound gently to flatten each piece to an even ¼-inch thickness. Season the chicken with ½ teaspoon of the salt and ¼ teaspoon of the pepper.
2. In a large nonstick skillet, heat the oil over medium heat. Add the shallots and cook until softened, about 3 minutes. Add the mushrooms, remaining ½ teaspoon salt and ¼ teaspoon pepper. Cook, stirring frequently, until softened, 3 to 4 minutes.
3. Increase the heat to medium-high. Add the chicken broth, lemon juice and thyme and cook until almost all the liquid is absorbed, 10 to 12 minutes.
4. Meanwhile, coat a large nonstick skillet with vegetable cooking spray and heat over medium heat. Add the chicken to the skillet and cook, turning once, until browned outside and white throughout but still juicy, 5 to 7 minutes.
5. Place the chicken on 4 serving plates. Spoon the mushrooms over the chicken and serve.

Calories: 202	Protein: 30 gm	Total Fat: 5 gm
Saturated Fat: 1 gm	Cholesterol: 66 mg	Carbohydrates: 10 gm
Sodium: 639 mg		

A SUPER SOURCE OF:

Phosphorus	▬▬▬▬▬▬▬ 41%
Riboflavin	▬▬▬▬▬▬▬▬ 51%
Niacin	▬▬▬▬▬▬▬▬▬▬▬▬▬▬ 99%

0%	U.S. Recommended Daily Allowance	100%

Thai-Style Chicken and Basil

4 SERVINGS

2 teaspoons vegetable oil
2 scallions, chopped
3 garlic cloves, minced
1 tablespoon minced fresh ginger
2 fresh red chiles, seeded and thinly sliced, or ½ teaspoon
   crushed hot pepper flakes
2 cups fresh basil leaves
1 pound ground chicken
1 tablespoon fish sauce (nam pla)*
1 tablespoon fresh lime juice
1 teaspoon reduced-sodium soy sauce
1 teaspoon sugar
Romaine or iceberg lettuce

1. In a large nonstick skillet, heat the oil over medium-high heat. Add the scallions, garlic, ginger and chiles. Cook, stirring constantly, 1 minute. Add the basil leaves and cook, stirring constantly, until the leaves are wilted, 1 to 2 minutes.

2. Add the chicken and cook, breaking up any lumps with the back of a spoon until no longer pink, about 3 minutes. Add the fish sauce, lime juice, soy sauce and sugar. Cook, stirring, 2 minutes. Spoon into lettuce leaves and eat out of hand.

Calories: 240	Protein: 22 gm	Total Fat: 13 gm
Saturated Fat: 3 gm	Cholesterol: 94 mg	Carbohydrates: 9 gm
Sodium: 146 mg		

A SUPER SOURCE OF:

Calcium	——————	23%
Vitamin A	———————	30%
Niacin	——————	27%
Vitamin C	——————	23%

0%   U.S. Recommended Daily Allowance   100%

*Nam pla, a fermented fish sauce of Thai origin (also called nuoc nam), is available in Oriental groceries and in the Oriental section of some supermarkets. If unavailable, mash 1 anchovy fillet mixed with 2 teaspoons reduced-sodium soy sauce and 1 teaspoon water.

PERFECTLY POACHED

Poaching is the technique of cooking foods by immersing them in a barely simmering liquid, which ensures, in the case of chicken, a moist, tender texture. It's also healthy because it requires no fat.

Timing and temperature are crucial. The liquid should be hot enough to cook the chicken through, but it should not be boiling, because extreme high heat and overcooking will result in a tough texture.

Heat the liquid—in the case of these recipes, water or chicken broth—to simmering. Immerse the chicken so it's covered completely by at least 1 inch of the liquid. Skinless, boneless chicken breasts cook in 7 to 10 minutes. Skinless, boneless chicken thighs take 12 to 15 minutes to cook. The meat should be white to the center with no trace of pink, but still moist. Remove chicken with a slotted spoon from its poaching liquid and loosely cover until it is cool enough to handle.

Poached chicken is used throughout the book in soups, salads and sandwiches. Here it is the star, used as a foil for spiced nectarine chutney, refreshing mango-mint salsa and the classic rich mole sauce of Mexico, made with chocolate, pumpkin seeds and spices.

*P*oached Chicken with Watercress Sauce

4 SERVINGS

½ cup nonfat plain yogurt
¾ cup chopped watercress
1 tablespoon minced scallion
½ teaspoon coarse grainy mustard
½ teaspoon salt
¼ teaspoon freshly ground pepper
4 skinless, boneless chicken breast halves (4 ounces each)

1. In a small bowl, combine the yogurt, watercress, scallion, mustard, salt and pepper. Stir to blend.
2. Place the chicken in a large skillet. Add water to cover and heat to a simmer. Reduce the heat to low and poach, uncovered, until the chicken is white throughout, 7 to 9 minutes. Remove the chicken, cover loosely and let stand to cool slightly. Serve warm, at room temperature or chilled, with the watercress sauce on the side.

Calories: 143   Protein: 28 gm   Total Fat: 1 gm
Saturated Fat: 0 gm   Cholesterol: 66 mg   Carbohydrates: 2 gm
Sodium: 378 mg

A SUPER SOURCE OF:
Phosphorus ━━━━━━━ 27%
Niacin ━━━━━━━━━━━━━━ 64%

└─   ─┘
0%   U.S. Recommended Daily Allowance   100%

Limit your sodium intake to below 3,000 milligrams a day. A teaspoon of salt is about 2,200 milligrams.

Cold Poached Chicken with Citrus Sauce

4 SERVINGS

¼ *cup red currant jelly*
2 *tablespoons finely chopped shallots*
2 *tablespoons fresh orange juice*
2 *tablespoons fresh lemon juice*
1 *tablespoon fresh lime juice*
1 *tablespoon port wine or marsala*
¼ *teaspoon ground ginger*
Julienne strips of orange, lemon and lime zest from half an
   orange, lemon and lime
4 *skinless, boneless chicken breast halves (4 ounces each)*

1. In a small noncorrosive saucepan, heat all the ingredients except the chicken to boiling over medium heat. Remove from the heat. Let cool to room temperature, then refrigerate until cold.
2. Place the chicken in a large skillet. Add water to cover and heat to a simmer. Reduce the heat to low and poach, uncovered, until the chicken is white throughout, 7 to 9 minutes. Remove the chicken, cover loosely and let stand until cool. Serve with the citrus sauce.

Calories: 190   Protein: 26 gm   Total Fat: 1 gm
Saturated Fat: 0 gm   Cholesterol: 66 mg   Carbohydrates: 17 gm
Sodium: 78 mg

A SUPER SOURCE OF:
Phosphorus   ━━━━━━ 23%
Niacin   ━━━━━━━━━━━━━━━━━━ 64%
Vitamin C   ━━━━━━ 23%

0%   U.S. Recommended Daily Allowance   100%

Chicken Mole

This classic Mexican dish, usually made for festive occasions, has been shortened to adapt for everyday eating without losing any of the rich complex flavors of traditionally made mole sauce. And instead of cooking a whole turkey, skinless, boneless chicken thighs are poached, which stay nice and moist. 4 SERVINGS

1 ounce blanched almonds
1 ounce hulled unsalted pumpkin seeds
2 tablespoons sesame seeds
4 skinless, boneless chicken thighs (1¼ pounds)
2 (5½-inch) stale tortillas, broken into pieces
2 teaspoons vegetable oil
½ cup chopped onion
3 garlic cloves, minced
1 jalapeño pepper, seeded and minced
2 teaspoons chili powder
½ teaspoon ground cinnamon
¼ teaspoon ground cloves
¼ teaspoon ground cumin
1 can (16 ounces) whole peeled tomatoes, drained, with
  juices reserved
*1½ ounces Mexican chocolate, cut into pieces**
¼ to ½ cup no-salt chicken broth (optional)

1. In a small skillet, toast the almonds over medium heat, shaking the pan frequently, until browned, about 5 minutes. Repeat with the pumpkin seeds, then the sesame seeds. Transfer to a plate to cool.
2. Place the chicken in a large skillet. Add water to cover and heat to a simmer. Reduce the heat to low and poach, uncovered, until the chicken is cooked through, 12 to 15 minutes. Transfer to a plate and cover loosely with foil.
3. In a food processor, process the almonds, pumpkin seeds and sesame seeds until finely ground. Add the tortillas and process until ground.
4. In a large nonstick skillet, heat the oil over medium heat. Add the onion, garlic and jalapeño pepper and cook, stirring frequently, until the onion is softened, about 5 minutes. Add the chili powder, cinnamon, cloves and cumin. Cook, stirring constantly, 1 minute. Add to the nut mixture in the food processor and puree until smooth. Add the tomatoes and process until smooth.
5. Return the mixture to the same skillet and heat over low heat. Add the chocolate and the reserved tomato juice and cook, stirring, until the sauce is smooth and dark. (If the sauce thickens on standing, thin with the chicken broth as needed.)

6. **Add** the chicken to the sauce and cook over low heat just until hot. Serve with white rice.

Calories: 415   Protein: 35 gm   Total Fat: 20 gm
Saturated Fat: 5 gm   Cholesterol: 118 mg   Carbohydrates: 27 gm
Sodium: 350 mg

A SUPER SOURCE OF:

Phosphorus	39%
Iron	26%
Vitamin A	25%
Thiamin	21%
Riboflavin	25%
Niacin	57%
Vitamin C	57%

0%   U.S. Recommended Daily Allowance   100%

*Mexican chocolate, usually sold in round tablets, can be found in Mexican groceries or the Spanish section of some supermarkets.

Chicken with Beet Puree and Horseradish Sauce

This dish is as rich in flavor as it is low in fat. Yogurt is the base for the horseradish sauce, buttermilk the base for beet puree, a cool, refreshing foil for the bite of the sauce. 4 SERVINGS

1½ pounds fresh beets
2 tablespoons buttermilk
2 tablespoons nonfat plain yogurt
2 tablespoons fresh orange juice
½ teaspoon salt
¼ teaspoon freshly ground pepper
4 skinless, boneless chicken breast halves (4 ounces each)
Horseradish Sauce (recipe follows)

1. Place the beets in a medium saucepan with enough water to cover. Bring to a boil over medium heat. Cook until tender, 30 to 40 minutes; drain. When cool enough to handle, peel.
2. In a food processor, combine the beets, buttermilk, yogurt, orange juice, salt and pepper. Puree until smooth.
3. Place the chicken in a large skillet. Add water to cover and heat to a simmer. Reduce the heat to low and poach, uncovered, until the chicken is white throughout, 7 to 9 minutes. Remove the chicken and cover loosely to keep warm.
4. In a medium noncorrosive saucepan, heat the beet puree over medium-low heat until hot. To serve, spoon the Horseradish Sauce over the chicken and the beet puree on the side.

*H*orseradish Sauce

MAKES ABOUT ½ CUP

½ cup nonfat plain yogurt
2 tablespoons fresh orange juice
1 tablespoon prepared white horseradish
2 teaspoons chopped fresh chives
¼ teaspoon salt
¼ teaspoon freshly ground pepper

In a small bowl, combine all the ingredients. Stir to blend.

Calories: 207   Protein: 30 gm   Total Fat: 2 gm
Saturated Fat: 0 gm   Cholesterol: 67 mg   Carbohydrates: 17 gm
Sodium: 604 mg

A SUPER SOURCE OF:
Phosphorus ━━━━━━━━ 34%
Niacin   ━━━━━━━━━━━━━ 66%
Vitamin C   ━━━━━━━ 37%

0%   U.S. Recommended Daily Allowance   100%

Poached Chicken with Mango-Mint Salsa

Salsas are Mexican sauces, usually prepared at the last minute, with chopped fresh ingredients. They are low in fat but packed with flavor and simple to make. This mango-mint salsa is a cool, refreshing accompaniment, with a hint of heat, to the chicken.

4 SERVINGS

2 mangos, peeled and finely diced
¼ cup finely diced red bell pepper
¼ cup finely diced red onion
3 tablespoons fresh lime juice
1 tablespoon chopped fresh mint or 1 teaspoon dried
½ teaspoon grated lime zest
1 jalapeño pepper, seeded and minced
4 skinless, boneless chicken breast halves (4 ounces each)

1. In a medium bowl, combine the mango, bell pepper, red onion, lime juice, mint, lime zest and jalapeño pepper. Stir to blend.
2. Place the chicken in a large skillet. Add water to cover and heat to a simmer. Reduce the heat to low and poach, uncovered, until the chicken is white throughout, 7 to 9 minutes. Remove from the heat. Serve warm or at room temperature.

Calories: 202	Protein: 27 gm	Total Fat: 2 gm
Saturated Fat: 0 gm	Cholesterol: 66 mg	Carbohydrates: 20 gm
Sodium: 77 mg		

A SUPER SOURCE OF:

Phosphorus	■■■■ 24%
Vitamin A	■■■■■■■■■■■■■■■ 89%
Niacin	■■■■■■■■■■■ 67%
Vitamin C	■■■■■■■■■■■■■■■ 93%

0%   U.S. Recommended Daily Allowance   100%

Cold Poached Chicken with Fresh Nectarine Chutney

4 SERVINGS

½ pound nectarines, peeled, pitted and diced (about 1½ cups)
1 small red bell pepper, diced (about ½ cup)
½ cup chopped onion
⅓ cup golden raisins
¼ cup packed light brown sugar
¼ cup cider vinegar
1 jalapeño pepper, seeded and minced, or ¼ teaspoon cayenne pepper
1 cinnamon stick
1½ teaspoons minced fresh ginger
¼ teaspoon ground ginger
⅛ teaspoon ground nutmeg
⅛ teaspoon ground allspice
4 skinless, boneless chicken breast halves (4 ounces each)

1. In a medium saucepan, heat all the ingredients except the chicken to boiling over medium heat, stirring to dissolve the brown sugar. Reduce the heat and simmer until thickened, about 30 minutes. Remove the chutney from the heat and let cool to room temperature; then refrigerate, covered, until cold.

2. Place the chicken in a large skillet. Add water to cover and heat to a simmer. Reduce the heat to low and poach, uncovered, until the chicken is white throughout, 7 to 8 minutes. Remove the chicken, cover loosely and let stand until cool enough to handle. Cut crosswise into ½-inch slices. Serve with the nectarine chutney.

Calories: 267   Protein: 28 gm   Total Fat: 3 gm
Saturated Fat: 1 gm   Cholesterol: 71 mg   Carbohydrates: 33 gm
Sodium: 65 mg

A SUPER SOURCE OF:
Vitamin A   ━━━━━━ 23%
Niacin   ━━━━━━━━━━━ 43%
Vitamin C   ━━━━━━━━━━━━━━━ 63%

0%   U.S. Recommended Daily Allowance   100%

LIGHT CLASSICS

We all have favorite dishes we remember from childhood that we still crave as adults. Eating healthy doesn't mean depriving yourself of these great favorites. With some smart substitutions, you can have your "fried" chicken and eat it, too.

Here Barbecued Chicken has its skin removed, and the oil is greatly reduced in the sauce, but the tangy sharp flavor remains. Chicken Paprikash uses nonfat yogurt in place of the traditional sour cream and skinless, boneless chicken to come in at an amazing 245 calories per serving, while its flavor is boosted and its volume stretched with tasty peppers, mushrooms and tomato. Skinned chicken thighs are coated with whole wheat flour, cornmeal and bread crumbs and "fried" in the oven, a technique that retains its moisture while it forms a crispy coating. Meat loaf simply substitutes ground chicken for ground beef or pork, and egg whites for the amount of whole eggs usually called for.

Chunky Chicken Chili

You won't ask "Where's the beef?" in this hearty version of chili, loaded with chunks of chicken and black beans. 8 SERVINGS

1 tablespoon vegetable oil
1 large onion, chopped (about 1 cup)
1 medium green bell pepper, chopped (about 1 cup)
3 garlic cloves, minced
1 fresh or pickled jalapeño pepper, seeded and minced
2 tablespoons chili powder
1 teaspoon ground cumin
½ teaspoon oregano
½ teaspoon cayenne pepper
3 cups diced (1-inch) cooked chicken (about ¾ pound)
2 cups crushed low-sodium canned tomatoes
1 cup chili sauce
1½ cups no-salt chicken broth
2 teaspoons Worcestershire sauce
½ teaspoon freshly ground pepper
1 can (16 ounces) black beans, rinsed and drained
½ to 1 cup nonfat plain yogurt
½ cup chopped red onion

1. In a Dutch oven, heat the oil over medium heat. Add the onion, bell pepper, garlic and jalapeño pepper. Cook, stirring frequently, until softened, 5 to 7 minutes. Add the chili powder, cumin, oregano and cayenne. Cook, stirring constantly, 1 minute.

2. Add the chicken, tomatoes, chili sauce, chicken broth, Worcestershire sauce and pepper. Heat to boiling. Reduce the heat, cover and simmer 15 minutes. Stir in the black beans and cook, covered, 5 minutes.

3. Ladle into bowls and garnish with the yogurt and red onion.

Calories: 237   Protein: 20 gm   Total Fat: 6 gm
Saturated Fat: 1 gm   Cholesterol: 38 mg   Carbohydrates: 27 gm
Sodium: 779 mg

A SUPER SOURCE OF:
Vitamin A   ━━━━━━━━━ 33%
Niacin   ━━━━━━━ 29%
Vitamin C   ━━━━━━━━━━━━━━ 68%

0%   U.S. Recommended Daily Allowance   100%

Chicken Meat Loaf

8 SERVINGS

2 teaspoons vegetable oil
1 large onion, finely chopped
1 medium green bell pepper, chopped
2 garlic cloves, minced
1½ pounds ground chicken
½ cup plain dry bread crumbs
1 large egg
1 large egg white
¼ cup no-salt chicken broth
1 teaspoon Worcestershire sauce
1 teaspoon Dijon mustard
1 teaspoon dried thyme leaves
½ teaspoon salt
¼ teaspoon freshly ground pepper
¼ teaspoon ground nutmeg
Dijon Mustard Sauce (recipe follows)

1. Preheat the oven to 350 degrees. Coat a 9 × 5 × 3-inch loaf pan with vegetable cooking spray.

2. In a medium nonstick skillet, heat the oil over medium heat. Add the onion, bell pepper and garlic and cook, stirring frequently, until softened, 5 to 7 minutes. Remove from the heat and let cool slightly.

3. In a large bowl, combine the ground chicken, onion-pepper mixture, bread crumbs, whole egg, egg white, chicken stock, Worcestershire sauce, mustard, thyme, salt, pepper and nutmeg. Stir until well mixed.

4. Spoon the ground chicken mixture into the pan; smooth the top. Spread half the mustard sauce over the top and bake 45 minutes. Remove from the oven and spread the remaining sauce on top. Bake 15 minutes longer, or until hot and bubbly. Let cool slightly before slicing.

Dijon Mustard Sauce

MAKES ABOUT ⅓ CUP

3 tablespoons ketchup
2 tablespoons dark brown sugar
1 tablespoon Dijon mustard
1 tablespoon cider vinegar

In a small bowl, combine all the ingredients. Stir until blended.

Calories: 213	Protein: 17 gm	Total Fat: 10 gm
Saturated Fat: 2 gm	Cholesterol: 97 mg	Carbohydrates: 12 gm
Sodium: 419 mg		

A SUPER SOURCE OF:
Vitamin C ━━━━━━ 27%

0%   U.S. Recommended Daily Allowance   100%

Chicken Corn Pudding

4 SERVINGS

1 teaspoon vegetable oil
¼ cup sliced scallions
1 teaspoon chili powder
¼ teaspoon cayenne pepper
½ pound ground chicken
1 whole large egg
1 large egg white
¾ cup corn kernels
¾ cup nonfat plain yogurt
½ cup skim milk
1 can (4 ounces) chopped chiles
3 ounces reduced-fat Monterey Jack cheese, shredded
¼ cup yellow cornmeal
1 teaspoon baking powder
¼ teaspoon salt
¼ teaspoon freshly ground pepper

1. Preheat the oven to 375 degrees. Coat a 1-quart round baking dish with vegetable cooking spray.

2. In a large nonstick skillet, heat the oil over medium heat. Add the scallions and cook, stirring constantly, 2 minutes. Stir in the chili powder and cayenne and cook, stirring, 1 minute. Add the chicken and cook, breaking up any lumps with the back of a spoon, until no longer pink, about 5 minutes. Transfer to a large bowl; let cool slightly.

3. Lightly beat together the whole egg and egg white. Add to the chicken mixture. Add the corn, yogurt, milk, chiles, cheese, cornmeal, baking powder, salt and pepper. Mix until well blended. Spoon into the prepared baking dish and bake until a skewer inserted in the center comes out clean, 45 to 50 minutes.

Calories: 283	Protein: 24 gm	Total Fat: 12 gm
Saturated Fat: 4 gm	Cholesterol: 117 mg	Carbohydrates: 20 gm
Sodium: 685 mg		

A SUPER SOURCE OF:

Calcium ━━━━━━━ 39%
Phosphorus ━━━━━ 24%
Vitamin A ━━━━━ 26%
Riboflavin ━━━━━ 28%
Vitamin C ━━━━━━━ 45%

0%   U.S. Recommended Daily Allowance   100%

Crispy Oven-Fried Chicken

Skinned chicken thighs are dipped in buttermilk spiked with hot pepper sauce, coated with a mixture of whole wheat flour, bread crumbs and cornmeal, then baked in the oven to as crisp a finish as any chicken fried in a skillet. Great to make ahead to take on picnics. 6 SERVINGS

½ cup buttermilk
½ teaspoon hot pepper sauce
½ cup whole wheat flour
2 tablespoons plain dry bread crumbs
2 tablespoons cornmeal
½ teaspoon salt
¼ teaspoon freshly ground pepper
¼ teaspoon paprika
1 tablespoon unsalted butter, melted
1 garlic clove, crushed
6 skinless chicken thighs (about 2 pounds)

1. Preheat the oven to 400 degrees. Coat a baking pan large enough to hold the thighs in a single layer with vegetable cooking spray.
2. In a medium bowl, combine the buttermilk and hot sauce.
3. On a large flat plate, combine the whole wheat flour, bread crumbs, cornmeal, salt, pepper and paprika.
4. In a small bowl, combine the melted butter and garlic.
5. Dip each chicken thigh in the buttermilk mixture, then dredge in the flour mixture to coat. Place in the prepared pan in a single layer. Drizzle the butter mixture over the chicken. Bake until golden brown and crispy, about 45 minutes. Serve hot or at room temperature.

Calories: 210	Protein: 24 gm	Total Fat: 7 gm
Saturated Fat: 2 gm	Cholesterol: 98 mg	Carbohydrates: 12 gm
Sodium: 326 mg		

A SUPER SOURCE OF:

| Phosphorus | ━━━━ 25% | |
| Niacin | ━━━━━━ 39% | |

0%   U.S. Recommended Daily Allowance   100%

Barbecued Chicken

4 SERVINGS

2 teaspoons vegetable oil
1 large onion, chopped (about 1 cup)
1 cup ketchup
½ cup no-salt chicken broth
3 tablespoons cider vinegar
2 tablespoons dark brown sugar
1 tablespoon fresh lemon juice
1½ teaspoons Worcestershire sauce
2 teaspoons Dijon mustard
3 garlic cloves, crushed
½ teaspoon freshly ground pepper
¼ teaspoon hot pepper sauce
8 skinless chicken thighs (about 1½ pounds)

1. Preheat the oven to 400 degrees. In a large nonstick skillet, heat the oil over medium heat. Add the onion and cook, stirring frequently, until softened, about 5 minutes. Add the ketchup, chicken broth, vinegar, brown sugar, lemon juice, Worcestershire sauce, mustard, garlic, pepper and hot sauce. Heat to boiling; let boil 2 minutes.
2. Arrange the chicken in a single layer on a foil-lined broiler pan. Pour the sauce over the chicken and bake, basting with the pan drippings, until the chicken is cooked through, 30 to 35 minutes.
3. Preheat the broiler. Transfer the chicken to the broiler and broil 4 inches from the heat until glazed, about 3 minutes. Serve hot or at room temperature.

Calories: 259	Protein: 26 gm	Total Fat: 7 gm
Saturated Fat: 1 gm	Cholesterol: 104 mg	Carbohydrates: 21 gm
Sodium: 733 mg		

A SUPER SOURCE OF:
Phosphorus ━━━━━ 22%
Niacin ━━━━━━━━ 40%

0%   U.S. Recommended Daily Allowance   100%

Chicken Paprikash

6 SERVINGS

1 tablespoon vegetable oil
2 large onions, chopped (about 2 cups)
2 garlic cloves, minced
1 pound skinless, boneless chicken thighs
1 pound skinless, boneless chicken breast halves
2 tablespoons sweet paprika, preferably imported
½ teaspoon salt
¼ teaspoon cayenne pepper
1 medium green bell pepper, thinly sliced
1 large tomato, seeded and chopped (about 1 cup)
6 ounces fresh mushrooms, quartered
½ cup nonfat plain yogurt

1. In a large nonstick skillet, heat the oil over medium heat. Add the onions and garlic and cook, stirring frequently, until golden brown, about 10 minutes. Add the chicken, paprika, salt and cayenne. Cook, turning frequently, until the chicken is lightly browned, 3 to 4 minutes. Add ½ cup water, reduce the heat to low, cover and simmer 5 minutes.

2. Add the bell pepper, tomato and 1 cup water. Simmer, covered, 20 minutes. Add the mushrooms and simmer until they are tender and the chicken is cooked through, about 5 minutes longer.

3. Spoon about ¼ cup of the hot sauce into the yogurt until blended. Then stir the yogurt mixture back into the sauce until completely blended; do not boil. Serve with rice or noodles.

Calories: 245	Protein: 35 gm	Total Fat: 7 gm
Saturated Fat: 1 gm	Cholesterol: 107 mg	Carbohydrates: 10 gm
Sodium: 316 mg		

A SUPER SOURCE OF:

Phosphorus	━━━━━━━━━ 37%
Vitamin A	━━━━━━━━━ 37%
Riboflavin	━━━━━━ 24%
Niacin	━━━━━━━━━━━━━━━━━ 75%
Vitamin C	━━━━━━━━━━━━ 52%

0%   U.S. Recommended Daily Allowance   100%

Chicken Hash

A great use of leftovers for breakfast or brunch. 4 SERVINGS

2 teaspoons vegetable oil
½ cup chopped onion
½ cup diced green and/or red bell pepper
1 garlic clove, minced
2 cups diced (½-inch) cooked chicken (about ½ pound)
1½ cups diced (½-inch) cooked potatoes
1 large egg, lightly beaten
2 tablespoons chopped parsley
2 teaspoons coarse grainy mustard
½ teaspoon dried thyme leaves
½ teaspoon salt
½ teaspoon freshly ground pepper
3 tablespoons skim milk

1. In a large nonstick skillet, heat the oil over medium heat. Add the onion, bell pepper and garlic and cook, stirring frequently, until softened, about 5 minutes.

2. In a large bowl, combine the chicken, potatoes, egg, parsley, mustard, thyme, salt and pepper. Stir to mix well. Add to the skillet, increase the heat to medium-high and cook, stirring occasionally, until lightly browned, 10 to 12 minutes. Pour the milk around the outer edge of the pan and cook the hash, turning, until nicely browned, 4 to 5 minutes. Serve hot.

Calories: 216	Protein: 20 gm	Total Fat: 8 gm
Saturated Fat: 2 gm	Cholesterol: 104 mg	Carbohydrates: 15 gm
Sodium: 374 mg		

A SUPER SOURCE OF:
Niacin ▬▬▬▬▬ 30%
Vitamin C ▬▬▬▬▬▬ 40%

0%   U.S. Recommended Daily Allowance   100%

FOR FINICKY EATERS

It is a challenge to come up with recipes children like, because they are usually picky about their food, and for many, Big Mac reigns supreme. Most kids go through a stage where they get fixated on a particular dish for a time, and the young ones tend to like their food very plain. I knew a little girl who went through a white phase. She would eat only white foods: pasta (with no sauce!), cheese and plain yogurt. And I can remember back when my brother existed on a steady diet of just hamburgers—never cheeseburgers—French fries and chocolate milk.

The recipes in this chapter make eating fun for kids, and the dishes are good for them, too. Ground chicken is substituted for ground beef in the Sloppy Janes, Tex-Mex Pita Pizzas and Spaghetti and Meatballs. The meatballs stay moist with a hidden ingredient—shredded zucchini, which adds healthy fiber with few calories. Chicken Nuggets with Honey Mustard Dipping Sauce are a nutritious alternative to the fast-food variety, and they take only minutes to prepare. Buttermilk Baked Drumsticks make great finger food, easy for a small child to hold. Baked instead of fried, they cook up crisp with their tasty coating of cornflake crumbs.

Almost all the recipes, such as the Chicken Tacos, include garnishes that can be omitted if your child objects. The recipe will still come out fine.

*S*loppy *Janes*

A take-off on the Sloppy Joe, using ground chicken instead of beef. 4 SERVINGS

2 teaspoons vegetable oil
⅓ cup chopped onion
1 pound ground chicken
1 cup tomato sauce
2 teaspoons Worcestershire sauce
1 teaspoon chili powder
1 teaspoon ground cumin
¼ teaspoon freshly ground pepper
4 hamburger rolls, halved and toasted

1. In a large nonstick skillet, heat the oil over medium heat. Add the onion and cook, stirring frequently, until softened, 3 to 5 minutes. Add the chicken and cook, breaking up any lumps with the back of a spoon, until no longer pink, 5 to 7 minutes.
2. Add the tomato sauce, Worcestershire sauce, chili powder, cumin and pepper. Reduce the heat to low and cook until the flavors are blended, about 10 minutes.
3. To serve, put the rolls, cut side up, on 4 serving plates. Spoon the chicken mixture over the rolls.

Calories: 344	Protein: 24 gm	Total Fat: 15 gm
Saturated Fat: 3 gm	Cholesterol: 97 mg	Carbohydrates: 28 gm
Sodium: 698 mg		

A SUPER SOURCE OF:

Iron	———	22%
Riboflavin	———	22%
Niacin	—————	34%
Vitamin C	———	21%

0%   U.S. Recommended Daily Allowance   100%

*C*hicken Melt

4 SERVINGS

2 cans (5 ounces each) chunk chicken in water, drained
¼ cup nonfat plain yogurt
2 teaspoons low-fat, no-cholesterol mayonnaise
½ teaspoon Dijon mustard
2 oat bran or whole wheat English muffins, halved and
*   toasted*
4 slices of fresh tomato
4 ounces reduced-fat Muenster, Swiss or Cheddar cheese,
*   sliced*

1. In a small bowl, combine the chicken, yogurt, mayonnaise and
mustard. Stir to combine.
2. Spoon the chicken mixture onto each muffin half. Place a
tomato slice on the top of the chicken, then the cheese.
3. Preheat the broiler. Place the muffins 4 inches from the heat and
broil just until the cheese is melted, about 1 minute.

Calories: 279	Protein: 26 gm	Total Fat: 11 gm
Saturated Fat: 0 gm	Cholesterol: 47 mg	Carbohydrates: 16 gm
Sodium: 514 mg		

A SUPER SOURCE OF:
Calcium   ▬▬▬▬▬ 27%
Niacin   ▬▬▬▬▬ 26%

0%   U.S. Recommended Daily Allowance   100%

Tex-Mex Pita Pizzas

These make a wonderful quick lunch or after-school snack.

4 SERVINGS

2 (7-inch) pita breads
¼ pound ground chicken
½ cup corn kernels
1 small red bell pepper, finely diced
1 scallion, thinly sliced
½ teaspoon ground cumin
¼ cup mild enchilada sauce
½ cup shredded reduced-fat Monterey Jack cheese (about 2 ounces)

1. Split each pita into 2 thin rounds. Toast in a toaster oven until lightly browned, about 3 minutes; set aside.
2. Coat a medium nonstick skillet with vegetable cooking spray and heat over medium heat. Add the chicken and cook, breaking up any lumps with the back of a spoon, until no longer pink, about 5 minutes. Add the corn, bell pepper, scallion and cumin. Cook over medium heat, stirring occasionally, 5 minutes.
3. Spread 1 tablespoon of the enchilada sauce on the inside of each pita half. Spoon the chicken mixture on the sauce. Sprinkle 2 tablespoons cheese on each pita half.
4. Broil 4 inches from the heat until the cheese is melted, 2 to 3 minutes.*

Calories: 200	Protein: 13 gm	Total Fat: 6 gm
Saturated Fat: 2 gm	Cholesterol: 34 mg	Carbohydrates: 24 gm
Sodium: 435 mg		

A SUPER SOURCE OF:
Vitamin A ▬▬▬▬ 25%
Vitamin C ▬▬▬▬▬▬▬ 52%

0%   U.S. Recommended Daily Allowance   100%

*Pita pizzas can also be cooked in a toaster oven. Top brown until the cheese is melted, 2 to 3 minutes. Or place in a microwave oven on a paper towel and cook on High until the cheese is melted, about 1 minute.

Spaghetti and Meatballs

6 SERVINGS

2 teaspoons olive oil
½ cup plus 2 tablespoons finely chopped onion
1 garlic clove, crushed
1 can (28 ounces) Italian peeled tomatoes, with their juice
¾ teaspoon salt
½ teaspoon freshly ground pepper
½ pound ground chicken
¼ cup shredded zucchini
2 tablespoons seasoned dry bread crumbs
1 large egg yolk
½ teaspoon oregano
1 pound spaghetti

1. In a large nonstick skillet, heat 1 teaspoon of the oil over medium heat. Add ½ cup of the onion and the garlic and cook, stirring frequently, until softened, about 5 minutes. Add the tomatoes with their juice, ½ teaspoon of the salt and ¼ teaspoon of the pepper. Cook, breaking up the tomatoes with the back of a spoon, until the sauce is thickened, about 20 minutes.
2. Meanwhile, in a medium bowl, combine the ground chicken, zucchini, bread crumbs, egg yolk, oregano and remaining ¼ teaspoon each salt and pepper. Mix until well blended. Shape into twelve 1-inch balls.
3. In a large nonstick skillet, heat the remaining 1 teaspoon oil over medium heat. Add the meatballs in a single layer and cook, shaking the pan frequently, until browned and cooked through, 13 to 15 minutes. Add the meatballs to the tomato sauce and simmer over low heat while cooking the pasta.
4. In a large pot of boiling, salted water, cook the spaghetti until tender but still firm, 10 to 12 minutes; drain. Place the spaghetti in a large serving dish. Spoon the meatballs and sauce over the spaghetti.

Calories: 406	Protein: 19 gm	Total Fat: 7 gm
Saturated Fat: 2 gm	Cholesterol: 67 mg	Carbohydrates: 66 gm
Sodium: 594 mg		

A SUPER SOURCE OF:

Phosphorus	━━━━	21%
Iron	━━━━━	27%
Thiamin	━━━━━━━━━━	57%
Riboflavin	━━━━━	27%
Niacin	━━━━━━━	42%
Vitamin C	━━━━━━	38%

0%   U.S. Recommended Daily Allowance   100%

Chicken Burritos

4 SERVINGS

½ pound skinless, boneless chicken breast
4 (7-inch) flour tortillas, warmed
½ cup shredded reduced-fat Cheddar cheese
½ cup chopped fresh tomato
½ cup shredded iceberg lettuce

1. Preheat the oven to 350 degrees. Place the chicken in a large skillet. Add water to cover and heat to a simmer. Reduce the heat to low and poach, uncovered, until the chicken is white throughout, 7 to 8 minutes. Remove the chicken, cover loosely and let stand until cool enough to handle. Cut the chicken into thin strips.
2. Place the chicken on the flour tortillas, dividing evenly. Sprinkle the cheese on top of the chicken, then fold the tortillas over to enclose the filling.
3. Wrap each tortilla in foil and bake until the cheese is melted and the chicken is heated through, 5 to 7 minutes. Top with the tomato and shredded lettuce.

Calories: 233	Protein: 21 gm	Total Fat: 4 gm
Saturated Fat: 2 gm	Cholesterol: 45 mg	Carbohydrates: 26 gm
Sodium: 340 mg		

A SUPER SOURCE OF:
Niacin ———————— 28%

0%   U.S. Recommended Daily Allowance   100%

Chicken Tacos

Arrange the garnishes in separate bowls so your kids can top their own tacos at the table. 8 TACOS

2 teaspoons vegetable oil
⅓ cup finely chopped onion
¾ pound ground chicken
½ cup corn kernels
½ cup mild taco sauce
¼ to ½ teaspoon chili powder
½ teaspoon salt
¼ teaspoon freshly ground pepper
8 taco shells
2 cups diced fresh tomato
½ cup grated reduced-fat Monterey Jack or Cheddar cheese
2 cups shredded iceberg lettuce
½ cup nonfat plain yogurt

1. In a medium nonstick skillet, heat the oil over medium heat. Add the onion and cook, stirring frequently, until softened, 3 to 5 minutes. Add the chicken and cook, breaking up any lumps with the back of a spoon, until no longer pink, 5 to 7 minutes.
2. Add the corn, taco sauce, chili powder, salt and pepper. Reduce the heat to low and simmer for 10 minutes.
3. Spoon the filling into the taco shells. Top with the tomato, cheese, lettuce and yogurt.

Calories: 182	Protein: 11 gm	Total Fat: 8 gm
Saturated Fat: 2 gm	Cholesterol: 41 mg	Carbohydrates: 15 gm
Sodium: 350 mg		

A SUPER SOURCE OF:
Vitamin A ———— 22%
Vitamin C ———— 24%

0%   U.S. Recommended Daily Allowance   100%

The amount of protein per calories makes chicken an exceptionally efficient protein source.

Chicken Nuggets with Honey Mustard Dipping Sauce

A fresh, healthy, delicious alternative to chicken McNuggets or frozen chicken nuggets. 4 SERVINGS

1 pound skinless, boneless chicken breasts, cut crosswise
into ½-inch pieces
¼ teaspoon salt
¼ teaspoon freshly ground pepper
Honey Mustard Dipping Sauce (recipe follows)

Season the chicken with the salt and pepper. Coat a large nonstick skillet with vegetable cooking spray and heat over medium-high heat. Add the chicken and cook, stirring frequently, until golden brown, 4 to 6 minutes. Serve with the Honey Mustard Dipping Sauce.

Honey Mustard Dipping Sauce
MAKES ABOUT ⅓ CUP

¼ cup honey
1 tablespoon low-sodium tamari or soy sauce
1 tablespoon fresh lemon juice
1 teaspoon Dijon mustard

Combine all the ingredients in a small bowl. Stir until well blended.

Calories: 196	Protein: 27 gm	Total Fat: 2 gm
Saturated Fat: 0 gm	Cholesterol: 66 mg	Carbohydrates: 18 gm
Sodium: 428 mg		

A SUPER SOURCE OF:
Phosphorus ━━━ 23%
Niacin ━━━━━━━ 65%

0%   U.S. Recommended Daily Allowance   100%

Chicken Cheeseburgers

Made with ground chicken instead of beef and reduced-fat American cheese, these are served on toasted whole wheat hamburger buns. Let kids garnish the burgers themselves. 4 SERVINGS

1 pound ground chicken
½ cup shredded zucchini
½ teaspoon salt
¼ teaspoon freshly ground pepper
2 ounces reduced-fat American cheese slices
4 whole wheat hamburger rolls, halved and toasted
Ketchup, mustard, relish and pickles as accompaniment

1. In a large bowl, combine the chicken, zucchini, salt and pepper. Mix until well blended. Shape into 4 patties about ½ inch thick.
2. Preheat the broiler. Broil the chicken patties 4 inches from the heat until cooked through, 13 to 15 minutes. Top with cheese and broil just until melted, about 1 minute. Place a cheeseburger in each roll. Pass the accompaniments on the side.

Calories: 322   Protein: 27 gm   Total Fat: 13 gm
Saturated Fat: 3 gm   Cholesterol: 101 mg   Carbohydrates: 22 gm
Sodium: 793 mg

A SUPER SOURCE OF:
Phosphorus ━━━━━━ 22%
Riboflavin ━━━━━━ 22%
Niacin ━━━━━━━━ 30%

0%   U.S. Recommended Daily Allowance   100%

*P*lum-Glazed Chicken Wings

Orange marmalade or apricot jam is a delicious substitute if plum jam is unavailable. 4 SERVINGS

¼ cup plum jam
1 tablespoon cider vinegar
1 tablespoon fresh lemon juice
1 tablespoon brown sugar
2 teaspoons reduced-sodium soy sauce or tamari
½ teaspoon ground ginger
1 garlic clove, crushed
8 chicken wings, separated, wing tips discarded (about 1½ pounds)

1. In a medium bowl, combine all the ingredients except the chicken wings. Stir to blend. Add the chicken wings and toss to coat completely. Refrigerate, covered, 1 hour.

2. Preheat the oven to 400 degrees. Place the wings in a baking pan in a single layer and bake, basting with the pan drippings every 10 minutes, until browned, 30 to 35 minutes.

3. Preheat the broiler. Broil the wings 4 inches from the heat until glazed and well browned, about 2 minutes. Serve warm or at room temperature.

Calories: 260	Protein: 18 gm	Total Fat: 13 gm
Saturated Fat: 4 gm	Cholesterol: 54 mg	Carbohydrates: 18 gm
Sodium: 157 mg		

*P*eanutty Chicken Pops

These pops are for real peanut butter lovers.   4 SERVINGS

4 skinless, boneless chicken breast halves (about 1 pound)
¼ cup smooth peanut butter
¼ cup no-salt chicken broth
2 teaspoons Worcestershire sauce
2 teaspoons cider vinegar
1 cup unsalted roasted peanuts, coarsely chopped (4
ounces)

1. Place each chicken piece between 2 pieces of plastic wrap. Pound gently to flatten slightly. Cut each piece into 1-inch strips. Thread each strip onto 4 metal skewers.
2. In a small saucepan, combine the peanut butter, chicken broth, Worcestershire sauce and cider vinegar. Cook over low heat, stirring constantly, until the mixture is hot and smooth. Pour the peanut butter sauce over the chicken skewers. Turn to coat completely.
3. Preheat the broiler. Arrange the skewers on a broiler pan and broil 4 inches from the heat, turning once, until cooked through, 3 to 4 minutes.
4. Roll each skewer in chopped peanuts and serve.

Calories: 395   Protein: 38 gm   Total Fat: 25 gm
Saturated Fat: 4 gm   Cholesterol: 66 mg   Carbohydrates: 8 gm
Sodium: 180 mg

A SUPER SOURCE OF:
Phosphorus ━━━━━━━━ 28%
Niacin   ━━━━━━━━━━━━━━━━━━━━━━━━ 95%

└─   ─┘
0%   U.S. Recommended Daily Allowance   100%

Cinnamony Chicken Chunks with Rosy Applesauce

I loved eating applesauce when I was growing up and all my friends tell me their kids do, too. My mom always made her own, and this is adapted from her recipe. 4 SERVINGS

1 pound skinless, boneless chicken breasts, cut into 1-inch chunks
¼ teaspoon salt
¼ teaspoon freshly ground pepper
⅓ cup unsweetened apple juice
2 tablespoons cider vinegar
⅛ teaspoon ground cinnamon
Rosy Applesauce (recipe follows)

1. Season the chicken with salt and pepper. Coat a large nonstick skillet with vegetable cooking spray and heat over medium heat. Add the chicken and cook, stirring constantly, until browned, 5 to 7 minutes. Transfer from the skillet to a plate; cover with foil to keep warm.

2. Add the apple juice, vinegar and cinnamon to the skillet. Heat to boiling, 1 to 2 minutes. Pour over the chicken.

3. Spoon chicken onto 4 serving plates. Serve each with ½ cup Rosy Applesauce.

Rosy Applesauce

MAKES 4 CUPS

3 pounds apples in combination, such as Rome, Ida Red and McIntosh, cut up
¼ cup sugar
1 teaspoon vanilla extract
¼ teaspoon ground cinnamon
1 cinnamon stick

1. In a large saucepan, place the apples and enough water to cover the bottom of the pan by ½ inch. Add the sugar, vanilla, ground cinnamon and cinnamon stick. Heat to boiling over medium-high heat. Reduce the heat to low and simmer, covered, until the apples are soft, about 30 minutes. Discard the cinnamon stick.
2. Press the apples through a food mill or a fine-mesh sieve. Taste and adjust the seasonings. Let cool to room temperature. Refrigerate, covered, until ready to serve.*

Calories: 356	Protein: 27 gm	Total Fat: 3 gm
Saturated Fat: 1 gm	Cholesterol: 66 mg	Carbohydrates: 59 gm
Sodium: 210 mg		

A SUPER SOURCE OF:
Phosphorus ▬▬▬▬ 25%
Niacin ▬▬▬▬▬▬▬▬▬▬▬▬ 65%
Vitamin C ▬▬▬▬▬▬ 36%

0%   U.S. Recommended Daily Allowance   100%

*Freeze leftover applesauce, in ½ cup portions, up to 3 months.

*B*uttermilk Baked Drumsticks

You won't believe these crispy drumsticks were not fried. The skin is removed, which cuts the fat in half. The buttermilk keeps them moist, and the cornflake crumbs give them a "fried" crunchy texture that will make them a family favorite with you and your kids. 4 SERVINGS

¼ cup buttermilk
⅛ to ¼ teaspoon hot pepper sauce
6 tablespoons cornflake crumbs
¼ teaspoon salt
¼ teaspoon freshly ground pepper
4 chicken drumsticks, skinned (about 1 pound)
1 tablespoon butter, melted

1. Preheat the oven to 375 degrees. Coat a nonstick 8- or 9-inch baking pan with vegetable cooking spray.
2. In a shallow bowl, combine the buttermilk and hot sauce. Stir to blend.
3. On a flat plate, combine the cornflake crumbs, salt and pepper.
4. Dip each drumstick in the buttermilk and then in the cornflake crumbs to coat, gently shaking off any excess crumbs. Place the drumsticks in the prepared pan in a single layer. Drizzle the melted butter over the top and bake until golden brown and tender, 30 to 35 minutes. Serve hot or at room temperature.

Calories: 148	Protein: 14 gm	Total Fat: 5 gm
Saturated Fat: 2 gm	Cholesterol: 56 mg	Carbohydrates: 10 gm
Sodium: 372 mg		

A SUPER SOURCE OF:
Niacin ━━━━━━ 27%

└──   ──┘
0%   U.S. Recommended Daily Allowance   100%

Chicken Parmesan

The inspiration for including this recipe in this chapter came from my friends Irene and Tom Nolan, who live in Brooklyn, New York. Their two children, Sara and Johanna, say it's one of their favorites. 4 SERVINGS

4 skinless, boneless chicken breast halves (4 ounces each)
1 large egg
½ cup plain dry bread crumbs
2 cups spaghetti or pasta sauce
4 ounces part-skim mozzarella cheese, sliced
1 tablespoon grated Parmesan cheese

1. Place each piece of chicken between 2 pieces of plastic wrap. Pound gently to flatten each piece to an even ¼-inch thickness.
2. Preheat the oven to 400 degrees. In a shallow bowl, beat the egg with 1 tablespoon water. Place the bread crumbs on a flat plate.
3. Dip each chicken piece in the egg mixture, then in the bread crumbs to coat.
4. Coat a large nonstick skillet with vegetable cooking spray and heat over medium-high heat. Add the chicken and cook, turning once, until browned, 5 to 7 minutes.
5. Spread 1 cup of the spaghetti sauce over the bottom of a 9-inch square baking pan. Place the chicken on the sauce, then top with the mozzarella cheese. Sprinkle the Parmesan cheese over the top. Bake until the dish is hot and bubbly and the cheese is melted, about 10 minutes.

Calories: 337   Protein: 39 gm   Total Fat: 11 gm
Saturated Fat: 4 gm Cholesterol: 137 mg   Carbohydrates: 20 gm
Sodium: 797 mg

A SUPER SOURCE OF:
Calcium   ————————— 30%
Phosphorus   ——————————— 45%
Vitamin A   ————————— 31%
Niacin   —————————————————— 74%
Vitamin C   ——————————————— 56%
⌞_____⌟
0%   U.S. Recommended Daily Allowance   100%

INDEX